LANGUAGE AND LITERACY SERIES
Dorothy S. Strickland and Celia Genishi, SERIES EDITORS
ADVISORY BOARD: RICHARD ALLINGTON, DONNA ALVERMANN, KATHRYN AU, BERNICE CULLINAN, COLETTE DAIUTE, ANNE HAAS DYSON, CAROLE EDELSKY, JANET EMIG, SHIRLEY BRICE HEATH, CONNIE JUEL, SUSAN LYTLE

(Continued)

Critical Passages

TEACHING THE TRANSITION TO COLLEGE COMPOSITION

Kristin Dombek
Scott Herndon

Foreword by David Bartholomae

TEACHERS COLLEGE PRESS

Teachers College
Columbia University
New York and London

Published by Teachers College Press, 1234 Amsterdam Avenue, New York, NY 10027

Library of Congress Cataloging-in-Publication Data

Dombek, Kristin.
    Critical passages : teaching the transition to college composition / Kristin Dombek, Scott Herndon ; foreword by David Bartholomae
        p. cm—(Language and literacy series)
    Includes bibliographical references (p.) and index.
    ISBN 0-8077-4416-6 (cloth)—ISBN 0-8077-4415-8 (pbk.)
        1. English language—Rhetoric—Study and teaching.   2. Report writing—Study and teaching (Higher)   I. Herndon, Scott, 1972–   II. Title.   III. Language and literacy series (New York, N.Y.)

PE1404.D656 2004
808'.042'0711—dc22

                                                                                    2003060802

ISBN 0-8077-4415-8 (paper)
ISBN 0-8077-4416-6 (cloth)

Printed on acid-free paper

Manufactured in the United States of America

11 10 09 08 07 06 05 04   8 7 6 5 4 3 2 1

In memory of
David Dombek
and
Robert Herndon

Contents

Foreword

This is the kind of book I love to read and to give to colleagues—a close, particular account of teaching, rich with student writing, classroom materials, and the implied voices of students and teachers as they enter and play their different roles in a semester-long argument on behalf of writing.

The course in this volume asks the fundamental questions: What *is* writing (and what might it be for those entering the university), what are its possible uses (both inside and outside the academy), and how it might be valued (what makes writing good, and good for *what*)? The course described in these pages was developed in the context of the distinctive and influential NYU writing program. And from within that program, Kristin Dombek and Scott Herndon have created an intriguing and compelling course, one they have designed and taught and presented to others, a course that negotiates the wonderful (and surprising) conjunction of grammar, theory, and popular culture. In the current academic market, books like this are few and far between. It is not a textbook, yet it is a book addressed to teachers and students. It is not a monograph or a book of theory, yet it reveals a serious involvement with scholarship in the field, and its argument presses upon a central concern in contemporary critical theory—the relationship of writing (including student writing) to thought and to contemporary culture (including mass culture). I wish a publisher or university press would develop a series of such books. (It might be titled: "The Scholarship of Teaching" or "Making Teaching Visible.") These are the kinds of books that are ideal for training teachers new to composition.

This book offers Dombek and Herndon's course as a course for the "college writing classroom," and I think there is much the field can learn from this rich example of local practice. The care and attention to the details of exercise and assignment-making is impressive and inspiring, as are the protocols for revision and the presentation (in a freshman class) of relatively sophisticated forms of cultural criticism. What I find most interesting in the book, however, is the attention to *form*, a term that has been pretty much lost to the profession (at least as a positive term) since the days of the Christensen rhetoric. As this book imagines students, they enter the college curriculum with "default forms" for thinking and writing—the declarative sentence, the thesis-driven essay, the conversion narrative. The problem is not that their writing is formulaic (writing is *always* a negotiation with form) but that (1) students have a limited repertoire of forms to draw upon and (2) they take form for granted or as an end in itself. The pedagogy, then, relies on *mimesis*—having students identify, name, and imitate exemplary patterns within and beyond the sentence. And it develops protocols for preparing to write and for revising prose whose goals are to identify evolving forms in order that they may be questioned, manipulated, supplemented, or challenged.

The authors say: "Throughout this book, we share ways of working with forms to generate new thinking, and ways of working with new thinking to generate better forms." (This sentence is an example of *chiasmus*, one of Dombek and Herndon's favored constructions.) In its concerns to promote both "process" and "critique" (how to write and what to say), composition long ago abandoned the sentence as an arena of primary concern. This volume provides a timely and important counterpoint; it combines a concern for cultural critique and the oppressive weight of standard forms with a sense of the sentence as a rich and crucial site of intellectual work.

From the sentence, the pedagogy moves to the "grammar of thinking, the syntax of ideas, and the architecture of the academic essay." To teach this attention to form, the course provides detailed exercises for students to follow as they prepare to write or to revise. And the book provides extended examples of students' essays—the products of this work. And the product is, as the authors note, distinctive, very much a part of the culture of writing at NYU; it is a "hybrid kind of academic writing." It is, as I read it, a form of applied "creative nonfiction," where narratives of personal experience provide both access to and a way of framing (and valuing) an assigned text, a work of high art or popular culture, or a particular problem in thinking. Students take their experience, including intellectual experience, as representative; as observers, they look for an image or moment in time that can stand, metonymically, for the whole. One student writes about his father, a Winslow Homer painting, and an essay by E.B. White. Another writes about the Columbine killings, Teva sandals, and the Christian right, with reference to an assigned essay by Nietzsche, "On Truth and Lying in a Non-Moral Sense." These are quite remarkable examples of student work—complicated, compelling, eloquent, and thoughtful. They are also, in the very best sense of the term, problematic. That is, they represent real work, work to be taken seriously; they are worth reading and, because they are worth reading, they are worth debate and discussion in our classes and at our conferences. There are very few books that provide us with such an opportunity, very few that allow us to think with such care and detail about the work of a composition course. And that is a shame.

—David Bartholomae

Acknowledgments

Our methods and many of our beliefs about how students learn to write, and teachers learn to teach, have grown out of our training and work in the Expository Writing Program at New York University. Thanks to its intense faculty development program, we have talked pedagogy with hundreds of other teachers over the years. As mentors in the program, we've observed the classrooms of dozens of teachers whose struggles and successes have intersected with our own and allowed us to design principles that, to the extent that they enable difference, extend beyond our own classrooms; we're grateful to the teachers we've mentored, who have mentored us, and with whom we've collaborated, for teaching us how teachers learn, and for sharing their wisdom and practices with us.

Like many teachers of freshman composition, our training originated in literary theory and cultural studies, rather than composition theory. The texts that have influenced our pedagogy the most come from these disciplines: Roland Barthes' work with the pleasure and politics of texts and images; Slavoj Zizek's writing on popular culture, desire, and ideology; Michel Foucault's thinking about power; Jacques Derrida's investigations into how texts work; Bertolt Brecht's theories on teaching and learning through performance; and the cultural criticism of Max Horkheimer and Theodor Adorno. Throughout this book, we turn to these thinkers for examples and support, in an interdisciplinary approach to constructing composition pedagogy.

At the same time, we have inherited intellectual mentors from the field of composition theory through our work in the Expository Writing Program at NYU, where we have been trained in a pedagogy inspired by a long line of thinkers, from the foundational work of John Henry Newman and Walter Pater to the rich debate between David Bartholomae and Peter Elbow. Our thinking is indebted in particular to the writing of John Dewey, Paulo Freire, Pat Hoy, David Bartholomae, bell hooks, Audre Lorde, and Joe Kincheloe, who have taught us that teaching composition demands an attention to theory as well as bedrock work with the structure of sentences, and to politics in the streets as well as in the university. For readers who are interested in pursuing this kind of pedagogy but would like more background and support, we've included a list of suggested readings in the back of this book.

For what is here, we must thank our students, without whom we would know very little about writing, and who have taught us to write and think in ways we could never have imagined. Of these, we thank in particular those who over the years have spoken and written to us at length about our teaching, helping us to do it better. And most of all, we thank those students who have generously given their writing to be read in this book.

There have been a number of teachers with whom we've been in close conversation about teaching for years. Our problem-centered pedagogy is particularly indebted to Ben Stewart, whose ways of working with problems have influenced our teaching, and our understanding of our teaching, immeasurably. We've been trained by five master teachers to whom we owe too much to describe here: Pat C. Hoy, who compelled us to believe that first-year college students can develop great ideas, and who provided the rules we keep and break; Darlene Forrest, who taught us how to learn from, and teach, other teachers; Mary Wislocki, who led us to new ways of understanding the learning writer's process; Denice Martone, who guided our work with international students; and Alfie Guy, who taught us to speak quickly, offer at least two opposing answers to every question, and have fun while surviving institutions.

To all those who have generously read drafts of this book, we give our thanks. To Stephanie Hopkins, for her incredibly thorough, rigorous, and encouraging reading, we owe a special debt. Thanks to Sally Stratakis-Allen, Sara Yff Prins, Ben Stewart, and Marion Wrenn for their readings, and to Carol Collins, Michael Greer and Lori Tate at Teachers College Press. To all the teachers and friends who have supported our learning about teaching and writing, too many to list here, we give our heartfelt thanks: Nanc Allen, Nuar Alsadir, Lionel Basney, Suzanne Bley, Dale Brown, Una Chaudhuri, Pam Cobrin, Kirk and Amanda Dombek, Nicole Heffner, Barbara Herndon, Kelley and Robert Herndon-Ford, Barbara Kane, Ari Kelman, Elizabeth McHenry, Lara Nielson, Jonna Perillo, Ellen Rowland James Vandenbosch, Margaret Vandenburg, Bob and Pat Weiss, Lejone Wong, Jon Wynn, and Lambert Zuidervart.

To Jen Weiss, muse and best friend, for her humor and love.

And to Alexander Kane, who makes all things possible, a lifetime of thanks.

Introduction

Writing is always hard, but for students making the transition from high school to college, it is especially so. Students are met on arrival by professors who expect different kinds of essays than those they were trained to write in high school. To complicate matters, expectations vary from discipline to discipline, and from class to class. For first-year college students, these expectations, and the reasons behind them, can feel as arbitrary as they do mysterious. Students attempt to accommodate these demands by means of a game of anticipation. Caught in a vacuum, forced to learn their craft before they understand the conventions and philosophies that structure academic writing at the college level, they construct a set of *ad hoc* methods to get by, trying to make the grade by guessing the values of their teachers as best they can. Among those who succeed at this task, many remain baffled by the reasons behind the demands. Too many do not succeed, and slip through the cracks.

We came to write this book because we believe that there are institutional and material reasons why so many students struggle with the transition to advanced academic writing. Too often, students and faculty understand these struggles as signs of students' inabilities, when in fact they are symptoms of a substantial gap in their writing instruction. If we can understand the nature of this gap, we can provide them with strategies designed to address not only the symptoms, but the deeper problem.

The institutional reasons for this gap are familiar to any composition teacher. On the one hand, our students' high school learning is directed by high school English teachers overburdened by the demands of steering their students through the SAT, applications for college, a host of achievement tests, and a state-mandated curriculum—teachers increasingly pressured to "teach to the test"; as a result, new college students' experience doing academic writing is often limited to reports, opinion papers, and Advanced Placement or five-paragraph essays. Our students' tenured college professors, on the other hand, are scholars educated in a rapidly changing academic climate, with new assumptions about writing, who often want to receive something different than the essays their students have been trained to write.

This gap between high school and college education is not, however, the same for all students; material factors intensify institutional limitations. Some students enter undergraduate education with a sense of entitlement to do intellectual work, inculcated in them by their homes and their high schools, and some do not. Studies have shown that dropout rates, in the first year of college education, are much higher among working-class students, students whose parents are not college-educated, and members of ethnic minorities. And so the lines that divide along class and race continue to divide in the first year of college writing (Clayton, 2002; Fine, 1991; Office of Educational Research and Improvement, 2000).

As first-year writing instructors, we find ourselves standing in the gap between high school and college, negotiating the needs of students of varying privilege. And many of us find ourselves there by necessity, not choice—as graduate students, adjuncts, or full-time nontenured faculty members supporting ourselves as we prepare for "real" jobs, or as tenure-track faculty required to do a stint teaching freshman comp. While we may not have intended to take on this responsibility, we are thrust suddenly and inadvertently into the point position, responsible for socializing students into the intellectual life of the university. We teach the class that will be scapegoated for students' later failures, and perform a paperwork-heavy job that demands much of our time but provides little financial compensation. The double bind of the composition teacher is precisely this: The class we teach is one of the most important ones in the academy, but our jobs tend to be marginalized by the institutions in which we teach.

For us, working and learning under these conditions provided a particular perspective on the gap between high school and college writing instruction, which offered us an unforeseen pedagogical opportunity. While giving students a crash course in academic life, we found ourselves in a prime position to develop new ways of thinking about the fraught relations among undergraduate writing, composition departments, and colleges and universities. Considering the position of our students as learners, writers, and thinkers from our own position in the trenches, on the underside of the institution, as it were, convinced us of the necessity to develop strategies for addressing the institutional and material gaps that shape our students' minds and their writing, without taking too much of the writing teacher's time.

Our central strategy for bridging the gap arose rather incidentally from the exigencies of being part-time writing instructors. As part-timers, we have worked in a variety of contexts and institutions, teaching writing to high school, international, "developmental," and honors students, for institutions that range from open admissions to Ivy League. Working in this range of circumstances has led us to discover similarities and differences among the ways that students with different kinds of training approach the task of academic writing, and to learn from the pedagogical approaches of very different institutions. Our work with both honors and developmental students has led us to ask what people mean when they tell us to "teach to the top" or "teach developmental writing." What does the frequently pejorative phrase developmental writing mean, anyway? Is slow and thorough work with grammar, syntax, and rhetorical conventions really in such a different universe from the "advanced" thinking that preoccupies us when we teach to the top? Can developmental writers only do important thinking once standard syntax is buried deep in their minds? And can students at the top learn to think better without studying grammar, syntax, and rhetorical conventions? We suspect that differences between developmental writing pedagogy and honors writing pedagogy sometimes serve to widen the gap between students positioned by their socialization to succeed and those positioned to fail, unnecessarily hurting both groups in the process.

If one assumption underlies *Critical Passages*, it is this: the student who has been through the battery of AP and college-prep classes can write better ideas given detailed work with grammar and syntax, and the ESL or dialect speaker can learn formal conventions better if invited to develop complex ideas and value their questions. Throughout this book, we share ways of working with forms to generate new thinking, and ways of working with new thinking to generate better forms. Such work, performed in our classes, can help teachers and students not only to learn but to understand the conventions necessary for clear, coherent, thoughtful academic writing. We refuse the false dichotomy that positions work with form as developmental and leaves thinking work to those who can speak standard English. Instead, we teach the grammar of thinking, the syntax of ideas, and thus the architecture of the academic essay.

The methodology we share in this book aims to reveal the forms that limit and enable our students' thinking and writing. Grammar, syntax, paragraph and essay structures, thinking patterns, and even the cultural structures we encounter in our everyday lives—all of these forms *make* meaning. Throughout the chapters that follow, we will show how the forms that allow us to express our thoughts, that structure the ways in which art is made and cultures are shaped, and that channel the ways in which we receive our communities and their creations not only make it possible for us to say what we mean, they make meaning happen. Our goal is to teach young writers to write confidently and well, by training themselves to see the forms that create meaning in their writing, in their minds, in the texts they read, and in the world.

Our strategy is first to lead writers to identify the default forms that limit them. What are the sentence structures they tend to use? The essay forms they repeat? The modes of critique they inadvertently employ? The attitudes that delimit their approach to the world? This initial naming, and the questioning that develops from it, will lead our students into work with new, challenging forms of thought and expression. The forms upon which we focus—grammar, theory, and popular culture—provides an unending supply of material for such work to happen. We investigate grammar and syntax because they create the basic limits on what we can think, and when we see how they do so, we can think in more powerful ways. We study paragraph and essay forms to discover the kinds of content they enable and foreclose. We share theoretical frameworks that can lend shape and rigor to our students' thinking, and help them critique the social and cultural structures in which they find themselves. And we turn to various manifestations of popular culture for the ways they reveal the forms of our lives, our attitudes—and, with some work, our best ideas.

In the first five chapters, we suggest a methodology for teaching students to identify form in thinking and in writing—to see the shapes and structures of good ideas, and create their own. We share strategies for performing this work with students at every stage of the essay-writing process: choosing a beginning thinking problem, finding sentence structures that foster and articulate ideas with grace, recognizing and employing the kinds of thinking moves that shape great essays, and reading and incorporating written sources. We end Part I with a chapter on revealing the structures of our teaching to students so that they can become their own teachers as they draft and revise their essays. In Chapters 6 through 8, we share ways of structuring content in the classroom to generate great essays, by using visual texts and other pieces of cultural production to teach students to identify and interrogate the forms of their own attitudes and beliefs, and generate new ideas out of that work.

Underlying all this is our belief that to teach students to think, we have to begin by helping them discover what forms their thought already takes. While this belief has important implications for teaching the conventions of academic writing, it also influences the content we bring into the classroom every day. You'll see from the examples we provide and the student excerpts we include that we tend to work with artifacts, events, and texts from popular culture, a content area in which our students tend to have expertise (which lends them confidence), but which has invisibly shaped their thinking patterns (the revelation of which can lead to new thinking). So we work with popular films, television shows, web culture, commercials, print ads, and music on a regular basis. Our strategy is to encourage thinking about those aspects of culture that our students tend to leave unexamined, in order to reveal to them the forms that structure their lives.

Working with forms in this way, we believe, is the best way to close the gap among students at all "levels." Revealing, modifying, and employing these forms for the entire class allows us to move flexibly between discussing grammar and high theory. And the work of making students conscious of their default forms, the way they've been trained, and what the expectations being placed on them now mean—all this puts the gap between high school and college at the forefront from the start, and enables an ongoing conversation about bridging this divide.

We believe that this kind of work with forms can help composition instructors to teach better and more efficiently, and students to produce excellent academic writing. Unofficially, however, we have another goal: to describe and argue for the value of a new, hybrid kind of academic writing. From what we've seen, 18-year-olds and beginning college writers of all ages, no matter what their previous training, can develop innovative and important methods for understanding the world—new knowledge—if their professors know how to ask them to build upon what they already know how to do. We believe that if anyone can think in fresh ways, it's the first-year college student: a person in a sudden period of exploration, new experiences, and, often, personal upheaval. The changes that accompany the transition to college can help to generate a kind of writing that holds experimentation and the ability to question as its core values.

The word *essay*, of course, means *to attempt*. And for the purposes of this book, we might consider essay to mean to courageously attempt not only to carry one's most complicated, new thoughts into writing, but also to see them through until they teach readers something. In this sense, though the common "pyramid essay," five-paragraph essay, and the type of writing we teach are all named *essays*, they nevertheless evidence significant formal differences. Our hope is that the kind of essay we teach combines the best of both worlds, for the standard forms do build a foundation for solid college writing: They teach crucial skills that range from ways of summarizing and arranging information, to bolstering straightforward claims with supporting points, to how to be clear and coherent. But considered at the college level, these standard forms are too simple and limiting to succeed in creating the kind of the writing we ask of our students. Advanced academic essays should require more: they should ask writers to pose rigorous questions and speculate about multiple possible answers, analyze several texts at once, sustain complicated trains of thought, wrestle with contradiction and paradox, and develop new ideas. Writing this kind of academic essay demands courage, because it challenges writers to value their own thinking enough to question and develop it, and to move from understanding others' ideas to producing new ones of their own. Such movement from reporting to exploring, investigating, and creating should characterize the transition from high school to college writing—and its difficulty should not be underestimated.

Teaching students to write in this way has influenced our own writing styles and processes immeasurably. We began to want to imitate our students' writing, because it got at things about the world that our own writing could not, and we began collaborating with our peers because we saw what rich writing arose from the group work our own students did. What was happening in our classrooms taught us to revise our beliefs about the kinds of innovative thinking that can be performed in the forms and ideas of rigorous academic essays. Unofficially, then, this book is not only about what we can teach our students about what the academy requires, or even what we can teach them about how to transcend what the academy requires; it is about what we can learn from our students about how to write better scholarly essays ourselves.

The structure and style of our classroom exercises, and the individual work we assign to students, draw on a model developed by Pat C. Hoy and elaborated by other directors and instructors in the Expository Writing Program at New York University. Over the course of a semester, we teach three essays—art, culture, and popular culture—each one initiated by a group of readings and carried out through a *progression*: a series of incrementally more complex exercises that helps students build up to an essay. Such a process invites revision and expansion at each stage of an essay's creation; as you will see, it also lends itself to extensive student collaboration. The progression model works because it pushes students to question, modify, and challenge their initial assumptions. It enables students to conceptualize essay-building as a constant process of thinking, reading, writing, and revising, rather than an intense period of reading followed by the overnight production of a draft. Finally, organizing semesters in terms of progressions enables teachers to hold rigorous conversations about content and form as they arise organically in the writing classroom, while the class's essays are under construction.

In Part II of this book, we provide three sample progressions that accompany our work in the classroom. They are intended to serve as models for how you might organize a set of exercises in your own classrooms, as you lead students toward the creation of their essays. Since the progression form relies on the incremental movement from one exercise to another, pulling one useful exercise from the group may not always work; we invite you to take what you wish, with the well-intended advice that your creation of your own weekly incremental model will be necessary to realize your goals in the writing classroom.

This said, as a whole, this book is designed to offer discrete, useful lessons in classroom practice. These methods are, in the main, what this book is about, and so we encourage you to read it for its practical ideas, its exercises, its prompts, its strategies for dealing with particular challenges that everyone faces as they're teaching writing. Our hope is that these will serve you well, no matter what kind of writing you want from your students.

Part I

THE STRUCTURE OF IDEAS

From Knowing to Thinking

> Each ought to move away from himself. Otherwise the element of terror
> necessary to all recognition is lacking.
> —Bertolt Brecht, "A Dialogue About Acting"

A few years back, University of Virginia professor Mark Edmundson (1997) diag-
nosed the current generation of college students for *Harper's Magazine* in his essay
"The Uses of a Liberal Education." By his lights, the overwhelming majority of
university students are "intellectually timid"—good at absorbing information, but
slow to question the ideas they study. Fearing failure, they seem "desperate to blend
in, to look right, not to make a spectacle of themselves"(p. 42). We begin with
Edmundson's perspective because it is typical. Walk into many faculty lounges and
you'll hear the complaint that despite our students' potential, they seem to hide in
the safety of the group, writing and thinking in ways that are too simple to support the kind of engaged, insightful academic essays we'd like to read.

Although Edmundson expresses a good deal of frustration with the students
who fill his classrooms without "changing the temperature," he does not blame
students for their lack of thought. Rather, he attributes their tendency to regurgi-
tate information and profess easy, clichéd ideas to what has come to be called "consumer culture." Characterized by the passive relationship between an audience and
the entertainment or products it purchases, consumer culture is a common scapegoat for students' failure to think, discuss, and write well. Certainly, our students'
experience as consumers does teach them to carry certain expectations into their
education, when they demand of a writing class, for instance, what a viewer wants
from a sitcom or a customer from a business: an accessible, concrete, easy fulfill-
ment of a given need or desire. Learning advanced writing requires skills at odds
with these expectations: active investment, delayed gratification, and an ability to
linger in productive dissatisfaction. So it's easy to treat consumerism as the enemy
to good writing.

But the problem of teaching writing is probably deeper and older than vir-
tual culture, mall culture, and even television culture. Good writing takes rigorous thinking, after all, and rigorous thinking is a difficult thing to learn to do.
Blaming consumer culture for students' passivity and simplistic writing too often
serves as a cover-up, when the real problem is that we do not yet know how to
teach our students to think. Do we know how to show them the difference between
reporting and thinking? Between a strong idea and a weak one? Can we teach them,
concretely and specifically, what good thinking looks like, so they can imitate it?
Can we describe the qualities of a rigorous mind at work? And can we do all this

9

in a way that is attentive to the learning process they must go through to learn to think—in writing? And even if we could, would we have the time?

These questions, taken together, make up the problem of this book.

WHAT STUDENTS BELIEVE

To begin, it's important for us to understand what our students already know when they arrive in our classes, and how they conceptualize the processes of learning and writing for themselves. The kinds of stereotypes teachers harbor about students make it too easy to assume that our students just don't care enough to work hard at writing. Our experience, however, has shown just the opposite to be the case: First-year writers strongly desire to write better, but often can't figure out how to do it. They tend to harbor fears that writing is inherently about talent, and that genuine improvement may be impossible for them to achieve.

We begin our writing workshops by asking our students to talk and write about what they know from their experience in secondary school. Here are some typical responses, gathered from a group of high school sophomores and juniors taking a summer honors writing workshop:

> Introduction. Body. Conclusion. That's how I've been taught to write. I sit at home for hours thinking about how I will put an essay together, rearranging facts before I even start to write. Format and outlines generally scare me. Outlines are supposed to help, but I find myself going nowhere with them. I always thought that writing was supposed to be the ideas and the style, but my writing classes concentrate on format. I end up writing horrible essays, at least according to my teachers' standards, because I write all over the place.

> I've been taught to write with an intro, thesis, body paragraphs, and conclusion. Writing has been mechanical. It is more about following a guideline taught in middle school and making sure all the components of an essay are present . . . I don't like the pressure of knowing my paper has to express the "right" idea.

> I feel that my writing has turned into well-coordinated phrases and quotes that slip together the night before the deadline. Teachers think my papers are well-researched and well-written, yet I know I lack the liveliness of others. My papers are like perfect picture puzzles ending in a nice picture at the end. I want to learn how to make them more complex, turning the puzzle into something harder like a 3D puzzle.

What do these responses tell us? These students are caught in a double bind, weighing their desire to express their thinking against the need for clarity. Interestingly, the tension between the two seems to arise from the forms the writers have at their disposal. While some feel stifled by the "mechanical" feel of "formats and outlines," others sense that it is in wrestling with the "puzzle" of form that a more satisfying kind of writing may appear. For some of our students, the tension may arise from not yet having mastered the form of the high school essay. But as our last example suggests, our students also sense that there must be better shapes for communicating their thinking, better forms for their essays, and a better relationship between their ideas and the structures in which they express them.

READING THE STRUCTURES OF FAILURE

How do our students' struggles appear to us as teachers? We doubtless share the belief that their thinking and writing can be improved. Usually, this belief stems from the fact that we are discouraged by the kind of work our students hand in early in the semester. Surely they are capable of more than this! For the composition teacher, there is always much work to do.

Imagining that you have before you a handful of first drafts, we'd like to invite you to reflect on the student essays that you feel are the weakest—the margins of which you fill with comments like "clarify," "doesn't flow," "connection?," and so on. In other words, consider those essays that seem to lack that elusive, exceptional quality of thought, analysis, coherence, or whatever you call it. But rather than concentrate on what these essays lack, think for a moment about what they *have*—the techniques they employ, and the structures that organize them. What rhetorical moves are these writers gesturing toward, in their attempt to achieve clarity? What forms and structures are they trying to replicate in order to make it sound like they're thinking? The patterns we can identify in our students' weakest essays can provide us with a guide to what they believe about what they're supposed to be doing.

In our classes for first-year college writers, the first assigned essay (after a drafting process of five or six weeks) asks students to develop their own idea, inspired by a series of readings they've done and an encounter with a work of art. These readings are essays by professional writers who work in a familiar, autobiographical voice. Our students are directed to choose one essay as a central piece of evidence and use their reading and interpretation of that essay, and of two or three secondary essays, to develop an idea of their own. We don't dictate the form of their essay, aside from suggesting that it should have a beginning, middle, and end, but we try to teach our students how to invent and construct essay structures and forms that best communicate their particular idea.

For many students, this assignment is a first attempt at a new kind of writing—one that develops an insightful, personal, and exploratory method of thinking rather than reporting facts or arguing for a commonly held opinion. For most of our students, in fact, this feels like a strange combination of the highly personalized "What I did last summer" writing prompt, and an attempt at a new kind of writing altogether. In this latter sense, they are right: We are asking them to bridge thinking about facts and intellectual arguments with the nonlinearity and personal engagement of the personal essay. Negotiating this gap by combining what are usually considered to be antithetical forms of writing is hard work, to be sure. It is so hard, in fact, that our students' initial attempts at writing essays are often incoherent. But something important results from these failures early in the semester: For the student, the grip of the five-paragraph essay has been loosened. And for the teacher, a crucial pattern begins to arise among those essays that fail. It is these patterns that show us what our students already believe thinking should look like; with them in mind, we can identify the steps they need to take in order to improve.

Below, we provide three of the most common structures that show up in our students' first attempts to write college essays. Though any of these forms can lead to successful essays, we are concerned with them here because they often serve as default formulas for writing, rather than platforms for thinking:

- Essays structured by an accumulation of sameness. In this common essay form, students seek to show that the truth that can be gathered from their primary text is exactly the same as the truth that can be gathered from the other texts they quote and from their stories from personal experience. ("Amy Tan struggled with fitting in at school, and so did Richard Rodriguez, and so did I.")
- Essays structured by conversion narratives. This essay seeks to show movement and change via a historical progression, but as a formula, it serves to offer an epiphany in place of a genuine turn of thought. ("When I was younger, I was scared of being injured or sick, but I read Leonard Kriegel's 'Falling into Life,' and broke my leg, and as a result I understand that suffering makes us stronger.")
- Essays structured as polemical arguments in support of a thesis. In using this essay, students marshal all their textual and experiential evidence to prove that their thesis is the only viable way to think. ("Our ideas of things are often different than the reality of them. This is proven by Plato, Jamaica Kincaid's essay 'On Seeing England for the First Time', and my trip to Spain.")

We will return to these essay forms and provide strategies for avoiding formulaic writing throughout this book. Here we are interested in them because of the way they function as formulas employed by students who are trying to make the grade. In conferences and on early student drafts, we see such a dynamic occur every semester: Students who are struggling to communicate in their writing *force themselves* to constrain their thinking in order to fit it into a pretty package, sealed and delivered to the teacher for an anticipated grade.

But it is not only the grade that draws students to default to these forms. In our classes, for example, students are explicitly directed *not* to write in these forms, but rather to find new ones that best express their questions and each complex nuance of their thinking. For the first-year college writing student, struggling with a new kind of writing assignment—an assignment that demands they demonstrate *thinking* rather than just reporting—we may wonder what still makes these default structures feel like the only viable option for meeting a teacher's expectations.

The answer to our question may rest in the issue of fear—or what Bertolt Brecht (1992) calls the "terror necessary to all recognition" (p. 26). What is familiar, simple, and safe serves as comfort against the unsettling, the uncertain, and the new.

Each of these forms tends to manufacture the appearance of knowledge at the expense of all that might threaten that knowledge—in other words, at the expense of thinking. At some stage in the writing process, students translate the demand that they produce ideas into a command to demonstrate knowledge and certainty. When we ask our students to make connections among multiple pieces of evidence, they believe they should show how all texts and ideas are the same (through the accumulation of samenesses essay), because the differences might threaten their sense of certainty. When we ask them to develop an idea from experience, they take the question as an imperative to describe a personal history that culminates in an epiphany (through the conversion narrative essay), because epiphany appears to be the ultimate performance of knowing. And when we ask them to make an argument that will have significance in the wider, public arena, they first make an effort to close out all possible counter-arguments (through the thesis/supporting point essay) because they feel they must protect their idea from any complexity that may threaten its appearance of rightness.

Whatever their strategy, students who default to these forms actually think they are doing what we're asking—showing that they know something—because they do not yet understand the secret we keep when we ask them to demonstrate thinking in their writing: *that we want them, actually, to explore what they do not yet know.*

The writing classroom can house the terror of recognition and the threat of the new; it must, if we are to lead students from knowing to thinking.

WRITING AS NOT-YET-KNOWING

In each of these structural forms of failure, students find ways to treat the imperative to think as an imperative to solidify thought into a one-dimensional form by cutting back on their own ideas or taking the path of least resistance through their reading. Because demanding that students demonstrate more knowledge and more thought often drives them to hide their excess or surplus *thinking* (i.e., anomalies, questions, and speculations) behind what they believe is a demonstration of *knowing*, we have begun to define good writing as taking that path which is able to sustain "not-yet-knowing."

This is the secret we needlessly keep as teachers and writers: Good ideas are born out of long periods spent without a strong, authoritative idea, and periods of having too many at once. This is a subtle but crucial belief for it suggests that a suspension of judgment (not a lack of thinking altogether) enables rich thinking to develop. But precisely because this not-knowing often feels to students too much like actually *being* stupid and confused (and stupid and confused is not something most students want to feel at school), it takes considerable effort and care to teach them to risk it. Fortunately, our students all have experienced the value of sustaining uncertain, exploratory thinking in their everyday lives; unfortunately, they may not think such thinking is appropriate in an academic setting. They may believe that academic thinking necessitates authority, and that asking too many questions destroys authority. We need to devise ways in which students can take their subtle, perhaps unarticulated thoughts and bring them into language, without rushing to an immediate conclusion or judgment. One of the first things we do in our writing classes is to help students to remember, by causing them to reexperience, the ways they already do the work of not-knowing—and to learn from this remembering some forms that can house uncertainty productively, even at school.

LEARNING FROM EVERYDAY THINKING

Early in a writing workshop, we spend a day showing students that they already know how to wrestle with a problem, without knowing the answer, until they come up with a good idea. We use this work to establish the class's goals for academic writing, and some of its vocabulary.

We tell our students that we are going to ask them to do a kind of writing they may not be used to doing in classrooms, and we suggest that they find a place in the room that feels private or, at the least, get themselves into a private state of mind. It is important to assure them that the writing they are about to do will not be read aloud, and need not be read by anyone, ever.

When all our students are ready to write, we give them this prompt:

> Think of one of your relationships—with a family member, friend, authority figure, boyfriend or girlfriend, whomever—in which there is a problem that you have not yet been able to resolve. Your assignment is to write a letter to that person in which you try to get them to understand the problem, as you see it, and explore ways to transcend it, or see it in another way. This is freewriting—don't worry about grammar or syntax, keep writing through any blocks you come up against, and don't be too critical of your thoughts as you go along.

Should you perform this exercise in class, you must be prepared for it to register a kind of shock. Many students are surprised when they are asked to draw the specific details of their lives into any classroom, let alone an academic writing class. In addition, the problems that arise in the minds of our students may be disturbing and difficult to address. After the exercise, we usually explain that by using this writing as an example, we do not mean to encourage writing for the sake of therapy in an academic setting. The goal here is not catharsis; it is to draw students to think and write about the complex world of a problem with which they are struggling for which there can be no simple solution.

We suggest that teachers write along with their students during this exercise. Though this may feel awkward, it can enable us to make contact with the discomfort of writing and enable us to take part in the discoveries that arise in the discussion that will follow.

We take 10 or 15 minutes for the first part of this exercise. About halfway through, we remind students that they should try to move from describing the problem to imagining and evaluating possible ways to transcend it. Something tends to change in the room as this writing takes place; it becomes quiet, and we can feel intense thinking in the air. When it feels like it is time to stop, we give students a few moments to quietly readjust themselves to being in the classroom— they need it. We might comment on the change in the room, asking students whether or not they can feel the difference between a thinking silence and the silence of busywork. (They always say yes.) By mentioning this change, we are already beginning to work together as a class to discuss what real thinking feels like. And now it is time to talk about what has happened, and what it has to do with the work of this class.

Reminding students that they should not talk about *what* they have written but rather reflect on *what it is like to write in this way*, we ask them to compare and contrast this kind of writing with the academic writing they usually do. (They don't know it, but in talking about "what it's like" without referring to content they are beginning to practice reflecting rather than reporting.) We keep track of these responses on the board, in a column for each kind of writing. Students are quick and prolific with their thoughts about this, so we'll just jot down a word or two to remind us of each comment. Typical responses run something like this:

This Writing	Academic Writing
• Personal, real, relevant, interesting—I care about what I'm writing	• Artificial, forced, boring—I do it because I have to
• The audience is real; it's for myself and the person I'm writing to	• For a teacher
• Thinking, trying to figure something out	• Showing I know something
• More emotional	• Reporting the facts
• Free-form	• Filling in a formula
• Learned something while I wrote	• Know what I'm going to write before I begin

Once students mark problem-centered writing as different from familiar versions of academic writing, a space is cleared for a number of questions. Out of the class's initial responses to these questions, we will begin to draw the vocabulary for our work together. For instance, we will push our students beyond what they perceive as differences between the personal and the academic by raising questions that explore and question the supposed boundaries between the two. What would it take for them to care about what they're writing about in an academic essay? When they read good academic writing, is it structured in a formulaic way?

Perhaps the most important question we ask, though, is about our students' assumption that their problem-centered writing is "free-form." We ask them to think again about that one, considering what kinds of syntax, diction, and paragraph shapes emerged as they were writing in response to a thinking problem. We direct students to identify, in their own language, the way their sentence structures become more complicated as they try to articulate thoughts they can't quite grasp: the way they find themselves wrestling with contradictory ideas in a single sentence, the way they pile on dependent clauses as they're rethinking something, and the kinds of language that surface as they entertain multiple possible solutions. In performing this exercise, students will also notice terms that demonstrate a reluctance to judge; they'll notice words like "but," "maybe," "then again," "what if," and "I wonder." They'll find that their writing is filled with questions.

What students have begun to name in this exercise are those choices that were made because they provided the best form for articulating a language of exploration: choices that range from diction and syntax to sentence and paragraph structure. What they can begin to hear, if they pay attention to these choices, is the sound of their minds thinking on paper.

If students don't say it themselves, we tell them: To write invested, interesting, and complex academic essays, they will probably need to develop a thinking problem as engaging as this highly personal one, marked as it is by no easy answers and lots of good questions. Throughout the workshop, we will return to, question, and develop three provisional principles about thinking problems that develop out of this exercise:

1. Good essay writing arises out of writers' engaged, rigorous, and creative exploration of a problem about which they do not yet know the answer. The process of doing this kind of writing can and should be demanding, certainly; along the way to being able to write new ideas about their problem authoritatively, writers may feel the very opposite of authority. Learning how to linger productively in uncertainty long enough to develop meaningful, complex ideas is at the heart of learning to write well at an advanced level. Feeling stupid, in other words, is part of the process.

2. Writing that manifests engaged wrestling with a complicated problem will break out of a thesis/supporting points/conclusion form, even if it is written in a formal, academic style. The order of things will be governed by the kinds of questioning and speculation being done. There may be a main idea (a complicated kind of thesis statement or claim) but one that does not emerge until partway through; an earlier speculation may be discarded along the way when new evidence is introduced; the shape will eventually take the form of the kind of thinking being done.

3. Sentence syntax and diction will change to accommodate the kind of thinking being done. Sentences in which a writer is wondering about relationships between two ideas in tension with one another, for example, will tend to be longer, with more dependent clauses, than sentences simply designed to declare a fact. In order to maneuver through these longer, more complex sentences, thinking language will emerge. The writer will begin to use phrases such as "I wonder," "What if," and so on.

After discussing these principles—designed to encourage engaged, speculative, exploratory, and complicated forms of thinking in writing—we practice finding difficult thinking problems to work on, rather than theses to support. Learning to identify productive thinking problems takes training; students can't transfer their ability to struggle and question in their personal lives to their notebooks and computers without a good deal of guidance and repetition.

EXAMPLES OF THINKING PROBLEMS

Let's take a look at two student exercises that illustrate what thinking problems look like as they begin to take shape in the essay writing process. In the first, Tori Shepherd identifies a conflict within her own relation to Britney Spears:

> While watching a recent installment of some flashy MTV show, my friend commented that one of her friends earns a living as a dancer for Britney Spears. He once told her, she informed me, that Britney wears a size eight

and often has to get her pants specially made to fit the curves of her hips. At first I laughed; no she doesn't, I thought, there's no way. My amusement at the absurdity of the possibility was quickly followed by a little tinge of hope—maybe this woman against whom the rest of the female population must be eternally compared really does have to buy something that is too big for even me to wear. Maybe that makes me better off than I thought. My laugh turned inward as I realized the folly of this idea; her eight is still a lot hotter than my six, right? Evidently it must be, for my continual oblique glances at the television whenever she appears reveal my simultaneously secret and blatantly obvious desire to look like that. Why wouldn't I? And why should I? What about this image has us so captivated and mesmerized?

The series of responses to Spears' jeans size that Tori stages here begins to articulate a thinking problem to which her whole essay will respond: Often women wrestle with a radical ambivalence about their relation to standards of beauty. This ambivalence breeds competition among women. But it also seems that women may uphold beauty standards for the sake of competing with one another. The image, in other words, may captivate us because we need to compete. As Tori continues on in her essay, it's evident that her thinking problem has begun here, in an invested and personal way, by reflecting on the problematic dynamic of her own desires.

In a second example, taken from the end of the beginning of Savannah Shange's essay on hip-hop culture and the problem of commodification, we see evidence of a student articulating the stages of a thinking problem in a more academic way:

> Now the subcultural phenomenon has become a worldwide market of competing images and profit margins; the political and historical roots of hip-hop have been submerged and a new truth is being sold back to the people. In his passionate dissent against capitalism, Karl Marx demystified the process through which commodities are born:
>
>> A commodity is therefore a mysterious thing, simply because in it, the social character of men's labor appears to them as an objective character stamped upon the product of that labor . . . products of labor become commodities, social things whose qualities are at the same time perceptible and imperceptible by the senses.
>
> Marx may seem to be discussing something unrelated, but understanding the invisibility of the hip-hop industry as capitalist manufacture is essential to analyzing the critical agency of its constituency. It is the product of our "labor," not in factories, but on street corners and vinyl—as documents of a newly born nation are co-opted by foreign profiteers. While we as heirs of the legacy of slavery in the New World can claim hip-hop culture as ours, born of our glory and oppression, too often we do not question the logic of buying evidence of what in essence cannot be sold.

Though Savannah's thinking problem is more academic in its tone than Tori's, it, too, develops a series of truths in tension with one another. Savannah has established a thinking problem that not only includes her experience of hip-hop in a theoretical frame, but will be capable of adapting that theoretical frame to her experience. Finally, Savannah's work sets the stage for a refined analysis and deeper questioning to follow.

So HOW CAN we make such work happen in the practical life of the classroom? Exercises 1.1–1.3 can help students to make the transfer from finding a topic to complicating an issue, and hone their problem-seeking and questioning skills in the early, conceptualizing stages of essay writing.

Exercises like these open the door to student writing that is messy—full of questions, going in several directions at the same time, plagued by paradox and contradiction. For now, we celebrate this kind of writing as long as we can see

---

EXERCISES 1.1–1.3

Exercise 1.1

Ask students to describe, in a sentence or two in their notebooks, an issue they're considering writing about. Tell them to draw a line down the page underneath this sentence. On the left side of the line, ask them to write everything they already know about the issue; encourage them to move from statements of fact (vegetables are good for you) to evaluative statements of which they are quite certain (being a vegetarian is more healthy than eating meat). Once they've written through the ideas about which they're already certain, ask them to fill the column on the right with all the things they don't know about their issue. They may begin with facts they're wondering about, but again encourage them to move to issues of judgment and, in this case, any lingering questions about the issue (I don't know whether it's possible to regulate the meat industry in any way that will work; I wonder if it might not be necessary for us to have a little violence in our lives). Discuss how the "not-knowing" statements and questions on the right side provide better starting places for thinking.

Exercise 1.2

Have students write a thesis statement about their area of focus that they believe would be supportable from whatever evidence they're working with. When they have finished, ask them to write five additional thesis statements, each one genuinely supportable by their texts. It will probably happen anyway, but as they're working you might suggest to them that they may discover contradictory theses supportable by the same texts; encourage them to search these out. When they are finished, ask them to freewrite about the questions and problems raised by the possibility of supporting all these theses, some of which are probably in tension with one another, from the same texts. In class or as a take-home assignment, ask them to edit this freewriting into a few clear sentences that summarize a problem raised by the collection of possible interpretations, and the contradictory truths generated by their reading of these texts.

EXERCISES 1.1–1.3 (*continued*)

Exercise 1.3

Have students list as many questions as they can regarding their chosen texts and focus. The questions should be genuine—things they're wondering about, having read these texts and thought about them. When students have generated a number of questions (aim for 15 or 20), a classmate will mark which questions would be answered by factual evidence, and which would have to be answered by thinking. Any students who haven't written questions that can only be answered by thinking should try to do that now. When all students have generated three to five thinking questions, have them think and write about the relationships between these questions. What themes emerge from the collection? Can these individual questions be combined together into more focused, complicated questions that could provide a center for an essay?

---

evidence that the students are working to complicate their ideas and explore multiple possibilities. In these early stages in the writing process, it's crucial that we support them wholeheartedly as they take the risk of delaying knowledge about their topic. By taking this risk, they begin to develop their own authority as questioning intellectuals, and the resulting confidence will show in their writing if we reward their explorations, however experimental they may be in these early stages.

The best way to generate essays that are problem-motivated, rather than thesis-motivated, is to provide students with texts that both stimulate them to develop their own questions, and serve as models for the kind of writing we want them to do. Every teacher should have a handful of such essays—writings that are accessible to students at the same time as they demonstrate rigorous exploratory thinking. It's crucial to sweat the details here as the class reads together—to develop a reading practice in the classroom that identifies the kinds of writerly strategies essayists employ to communicate thoughtful questioning, wondering, and idea development. In Chapter 2, we investigate some of the formal aspects of articulating excellent thinking as they appear in such texts. For now, it's enough to say that with repeated careful readings and discussions, students can come to understand that professional texts are not created out of certainty, but are records of a writer's sustained wrestling with a problem she came to articulate, and perhaps transcend, through writing. And as students learn to read texts as records of struggle, they will gain the confidence to "essay" on their own, with the authority that comes with being willing to not-yet-know.

2 *The Grammar of Ideas*

> To go upstairs in the word house, is to withdraw, step by step; while to go
> down to the cellar is to dream . . . To mount and descend in the words
> themselves—this is a poet's life. To mount too high or descend too low, is
> allowed in the case of poets, who bring earth and sky together. Must the
> philosopher alone be condemned by his peers always to live on the ground
> floor?
>
> —Gaston Bachelard, *The Poetics of Space*

In a break with the grammar-heavy pedagogy of their predecessors, most composition teachers now take it as a given that students write better when they're not focused on grammar, and for good reason: a myriad of studies has shown that grammar lessons do little to train writers to monitor for mistakes, much less improve their writing. This ineffectiveness is so well documented that the National Council of Teachers of English (NCTE) heads its fact sheet, "On the Teaching of Grammar," with a quote from a 1991 study by George Hillocks and Michael Smith that asserts, "Research over a period of ninety years has consistently shown that the teaching of school grammar has little or no effect on students" (Weaver, 1996). The fact sheet instructs writing teachers to teach grammar only in local instances, in individual conferences with students. Characterized through the phrase "process before product," an inversion of priorities has manifested itself in new pedagogy at all levels of English instruction.

The teaching of elementary school and high school English has been so transformed that most first-year students enter college with little or no formal training in grammar or syntax. But here a problem arises, for rather than writing with naturally fluent abandon, thanks to their lack of "error"-centered writing education, these students are often harried by a vague sense that there is a club of formal or grammatical "rightness" out there somewhere into which they have not been granted access. They generally deal with this sense of exclusion and inevitable failure in one of two ways. If they're brave or simply don't care, they write tangled sentences (and, when asked to revise, retangle them in ways that can seem arbitrary) or they turn to short, careful declarative sentences in order to stave off the red pen of the writing teacher, wary of the rules they know must exist but cannot name.

Perhaps for this reason, recent years have seen a backlash against the anti-grammar movement. Stanley Fish (2002), for example, has argued that the demise of good grammar can be attributed to these trends in pedagogy, which value self-expression over and against both grammatical accuracy and submission to the conventions of writing:

> . . . so many of our students are incapable of writing intelligible sentences or of link-
> ing one bad sentence to another in something that approximates an argument. They
> have been allowed to believe that their opinions—formed by nothing, supported
> by even less—are interesting. The belief that what you're supposed to do is express
> yourself goes hand in hand with the belief that whatever you happen to express is
> valuable, and if you believe both these things you will not believe that there is any
> reason to worry about subject verb agreement or pronouns without nouns or miss-
> ing transitions or anything else. (website)

Fish suggests that writing instructors should tell their students to throw out their
belief in content, to "Check your opinions, your ideas, your views at the door; they
are not fungible currency here," but he admits that it's not that simple; he adds
that "structural changes in the way writing and argument are taught" need to be
made to rectify the problems caused by the dearth of grammar instruction in recent years. His conclusion:

> Every dean should forthwith insist that all composition courses teach grammar and
> rhetoric and nothing else. No composition course should have a theme, especially
> not one the instructor is interested in. Ideas should be introduced not for their own
> sake, but for the sake of the syntactical and rhetorical points they help illustrate,
> and once they serve this purpose, they should be sent away. Content should be
> avoided like the plague it is. . . . (website)

    Fish's argument is organized by the same set of binary oppositions that have
framed the traditional debate over grammar instruction—old, crusty oppositions
that, because of their long histories, inevitably influence the structure of our
thoughts as we learn to write and teach. The binaries go something like this:

Content	Form
Expression	Communication
Ideas	Grammar and syntax
Opinion	Rigor
Disorder	Structure
Natural	Educated
Individual	Social
Student	Teacher

Horizontally, we find false oppositions; vertically, forced alliances between terms
that should not necessarily be equated. From Fish's side of the argument, which
values the terms in the right-hand column, these alliances position students as dis-
orderly and opinionated, in contrast to the teacher, who possesses the knowledge
and authority responsible for shaping the natural, expressive individual into a
properly socialized and structured thinker. For the anti-grammar side, which values at least some of the terms in the left-hand column, too much attention to structure, form, and rigor by a teacher is seen as opposing or limiting students' ideas
and expression. And both sides of the debate hang their arguments on keeping
content and form in an oppositional relation to one another.
    Although the gist of his argument pits form against content, Fish concludes
on a surprising note. He writes, "Content should be avoided like the plague it is,

except for the deep and inexhaustible content that will reveal itself once the dynamics of language are regarded not as secondary, mechanical aids to thought, but as thought itself." This is a perplexing sentence. If, for Fish, the "dynamics of language" are "thought itself," rather than tools of thought, then why should students check their ideas at the door in order to learn the rules of form? In fact, how could they? Don't their ideas (always) already participate in "the dynamics of language"? Doesn't student writing already possess its own form, grammar, and syntax? Is the point, then, that the only ideas that have good form are those of professional writers? And if so, how is it that the *content* of professional writing might be discarded, once the form has been noted, as Fish suggests would be best when he writes, "once they serve this purpose, [ideas] should be sent away"? If the form and content of ideas are inseparable, as Fish seems to assert, where will that content *go*, exactly, once it is "sent away"? Foreclosed in this way, won't such content return in the "thinking" students do in their own writing, causing them to repeat simplified versions of the ideas of others?

THE FORM OF CONTENT

In our writing instruction, we can refuse the double bind that would pit the study of the constraints of language against the smart expression of our students' ideas. There is no such opposition between form and content, after all—or rather, the opposition, to the extent that it often functions as one, can be productive and provocative, helpful and fun. To illustrate this possibility, let's take a look at the long paragraph preceding this one.

In analyzing Fish we challenged ourselves to write a series of questions, each one building on the one before—and because of this formal constraint, we ended up at an idea we hadn't initially intended to articulate (that when we fail to deal explicitly with the content of the model texts we read together, we inadvertently doom students to repeat the ideas of others). Asking our students to employ straightforward formal constraints like these can help them to generate ideas—content that they might not otherwise have discovered.

What are the chances that our students will come up with a really good question by the end of such a paragraph? In our experience, the chances are pretty high. Exercises like the paragraph-of-questions exercise, that work through heightening the constraints of language, tend to generate more original ideas. We do agree

---

EXERCISE 2.1

Ask students to write a paragraph of eight sentences in which each sentence must be in the form of a question. Each new question must respond to the question before it by posing a new complication, doubt, or possibility. Direct students to read aloud their first and last questions, and discuss the movement of thinking between the two.

with the assumption that has dominated composition pedagogy since the 1960s: for substantial parts of their process, writers should be given permission to write without the burden of perfection, particularly grammatical perfection. And yet grammar cannot be thrown away, for the converse is also true: Writers cannot come up with original and creative ideas and complex trains of thought unless they know the sentence structures in which to think. And so we must study sentence structures to teach us how to have ideas, and ideas to teach us how to have sentence structures.

CHIASMUS AND DECLARATIVE SENTENCES

The last sentence of the preceding paragraph provides a good example of a structure that forms content in a particular, idea-generating way. It has a basic chiasmus structure, wherein the two terms "sentence structures" and "ideas" are inverted, with the same verb group, "to teach us how to have," repeated. It is a sentence structure built for the kind of reciprocal thinking that tends to begin to break down binary oppositions—in this one, the content/form binary—and thus is a sentence structure that is already doing the work of complicating thought.

Chiasmus is a sentence structure for subversion, which is why Milton (2001) has Satan speak in chiasmi throughout *Paradise Lost*: "The mind is its own place, and in itself can make/a Heav'n of Hell, a Hell of Heav'n" (1:254–5). It is also a sentence structure that can uncover the absurdity of a phenomenon in a quick, direct gesture, as Charlotte Perkins Gilman (1989) does when she writes, "The women who do the most work get the least money, and the women who have the most money do the least work" (p. 141). And it is a flexible structure, a simple and elegant pattern that can be expanded to argue a point through a more complex inversion, as René Girard (1977) does in this loose chiasmus:

> If men wish to prevent an interminable outbreak of vengeance (just as today we wish to prevent nuclear war), it is not enough to convince their fellows that violence is detestable—for it is precisely because they detest violence that men make a duty of vengeance. (p. 21)

Student writing with chiasmus-shaped ideas is already hunting for complexity; because of this, chiasmus can function as a tool at each stage in the writing process. (In fact, we'll return to chiasmus later on to explore ways of using it to build main ideas.) For now, we will use it to show the interplay between form and function that should reshape our way of teaching writing.

Think of a parallel in architecture: When utilitarian philosopher Jeremy Bentham (1995) came up with his idea for a circular building with a central watchtower, he created a form that was simultaneously an idea, and an idea with power; in his prison, a warden occupying a central tower would have the ability to monitor any prisoner in the building from a single, hidden position. In Bentham's mind, the panopticon would create "self-surveillance" in its prisoners—a kind of thought content—simply by means of being structured the way that it was. Each prisoner, student, inmate, or patient occupying a room along those circular walls would imagine that they were being watched whether they actually were or not, and behave themselves. In comparison to the dank dungeons that preceded it, the panopticon was thought to be a major step forward in reforming the bodies—and minds—of prisoners.

The panopticon is a particularly powerful example of how a formal structure can organize its occupants and, in doing so, both enable and foreclose certain ways of living or thinking. Every sentence, too, organizes its content one way or another, and it is through this organization that meaning is made. Too often, the simple declarative sentence functions as the unrecognized prison in which many beginning college writers live; their thinking goes only as far as its form will allow, which is not far at all. The simple declarative sentence allows for statements of fact, of identity; its logic is propositional. To *think* in the simple declarative sentence would amount to creating a riddle, incorporating a surprise into the straightforwardness of the form itself. Such a surprise helps the content of the sentence transcend the constraining simplicity of its form in at least two ways:

1. by inviting the reader to figure out the riddle as it stands now
2. by convincing the reader that an explanation is on the way

It is perhaps in this first sense that Gertrude Stein (1975) achieves surprise when she repeats, in her book *How to Write*, the simple declarative sentence, "A sentence is a duplicate." And as far as the second type of surprise goes, Ralph Ellison (1980) achieves this effect by beginning his book with the simple declarative sentence, "I am an invisible man." Ellison's entire novel functions as an explanation of this ambiguous sentence.

Thinking is achieved in each sentence by the writer's consciousness of how the form itself works to create meaning in the reader's mind. Because the form is simple, and because these authors use the apparent simplicity of this form to create a riddle, readers are convinced that Ellison and Stein's work contains the spark of new thinking to come. It is this attention to form that we can inculcate in students by comparing and contrasting the work that simple declarative sentences do with that of more complex forms such as chiasmus.

CUMULATIVE AND PERIODIC SENTENCES

We do not tend to speak in simple, declarative sentences: "I went to the mall." Our everyday lives ask us to communicate more than that. We speak, generally, in "loose" sentences, adding on phrases and clauses with the help of conjunctions. "I went to the mall, and I saw the Seven jeans I've been wanting to get, but they were too much." The writerly version of this kind of sentence is the cumulative sentence. The base clause contains a subject, verb, and object, and begins the sentence: "I went to the mall." The cumulative sentence is constructed by adding modifying phrases after the subject, verb, and/or object. One can do so almost indefinitely. Consider, for example, the following sentence:

> I went to the mall, looking for the jeans I had to have, the jeans from Seven, the expensive ones, the best pants in town, my first real effort at becoming cool, an impossible feat, sadly designed to undo me.

In sentences like these, modifying phrases can begin in a number of ways: with verbals (looking for the jeans I had to have); with an article and a noun from the base clause (the jeans from Seven); with an article, adjective, and base clause noun (the expensive ones); with an article, adjective, any noun, and a prepositional phrase (the best pants in town); with a possessive pronoun (my first real effort at becoming cool); with an article plus an appositive for the base clause or the noun being modified (an impossible feat); with an adverb or article plus verb (sadly designed to undo me).

To be sure, the sentence we offer above isn't a great one, but it does succeed in modeling a range of kinds of modification. This is a mixed cumulative sentence in that some of its phrases modify the base clause, which is called coordinate modification, and some of its phrases modify the previous phrase, which is called subordinate modification. It is difficult to write a well-conceived cumulative sentence with subordinate modification without doing two things: first, without learning a bit of grammar, and second, without deepening your thinking about the base clause, thereby complicating its meaning. Because of the way it tends to generate thinking, the cumulative sentence is a great teaching tool when students are in the early stages of writing an essay.

Building a good cumulative sentence is very difficult, but we're not concerned that our students immediately get it right; rather, we want to make sure that they begin to feel the way that constructing subordinate and coordinate modification can help them to develop their description (and their interpretation) of a phenomenon.

We teach modification by doing it together with our students. First, we put a base clause on the board:

> Britney Spears is the ideal American girl.

Then we ask the class for adjectives, nouns, adverbs, and verbs that come to mind when they think of Spears. Once we have 8 or 10 words in each category, we ask students to put them together into phrases, and we piece the phrases together on the board until we have something like a sentence, teaching students the difference between modifying the base clause (coordination) and modifying the clause before (subordination) as we go:

> Britney Spears is the ideal American girl—the blonde, pretty one, with the cheerleader smile, dancing like a stripper, singing like a choirgirl, who only cries at home, in her palatial white bedroom, mourning her virginity, mourning what it cost her to perform for us.

Through the constraints of this game of description, we have created a sentence as a class that, because of the multiplicity of its modifiers, creates tension and highlights contradictions. Writing this sentence together helps us to discuss the contradictions present in any popular cultural icon or image—and, in fact, in any text we might consider—and the value of lingering on them. Only after spending time on the initial image can we really tease out the complications of the sentence. And similarly, the cumulative and periodic sentence structures can help us to practice reading images in a way that generates ideas for our essays. After constructing this cumulative sentence, we flip it so that we can teach periodic structure in which the main clause comes at the end of the sentence. Students like this better; it builds more drama into the sentence, they say, and asks the reader to do more work imagining the image, speculating on her own; they notice that this sentence structure seems to demand a bit more of an idea at the end of it, and that it has already set us up for a kind of idea, so we add it:

> The blonde, pretty one, with the cheerleader smile, dancing like a stripper, singing like a choirgirl, who only cries at home, in her palatial white bedroom, mourning her virginity, mourning what it cost her to perform for us—if Britney Spears is the ideal American girl, the American girl is a study in contrasts.

After showing students how cumulative and periodic sentence structures can generate thinking, we invite them to create these kinds of sentences as a way of teasing out the complications of the images they have chosen to analyze in their essays. Here is how one student, Candy Goh, uses a periodic sentence to develop a rich, detailed image in the beginning of her essay, which has built into it the tensions at the center of her essay's thinking problem:

> The perfect imitation of vogue. Short skirts, loose white knee-length socks, platform shoes, all kinds of accessories, bleached re-bonded hair, skin tanned to a golden copper, white-based makeup and glitter on her face, dancing with perfect rhythm and style to Dance Dance Revolution, carrying pictures and little items from her latest pop idol group F4, listening to Britney Spears and N'Sync, keeping scores of photo-stickers of her friends and herself in cutesy books—she is the epitome of cool Asian pop culture.
>   Self. Does she have one? She is a borrower. Nothing in her is original. She looks to Japanese school girls for her fashion and activities, Korean girls for her makeup, takes her cue from the Taiwanese to idolize F4, and scours American pop culture for music trends. Yet, she is what Malcolm Gladwell would describe in "The Coolhunt" as an "innovator.". . .

Note the way that Candy follows her long, periodic sentence with abrupt, short sentences, juxtaposing sentence structures to build tension and drama into the form of the beginning of her essay—formal choices that set up her essay's main thinking problem about how the superficial gestures of pop culture can serve to function as both markers of our personality and erasers of our individuality at the same time.

USING CUMULATIVE AND PERIODIC SENTENCES TO TEACH PARAGRAPH AND ESSAYS

Once students can recognize and imitate cumulative and periodic patterns at the sentence level, they can use these patterns to conceptualize the organization of paragraphs and essays. Just as students tend to write in simple, declarative sentences coming out of high school, they also tend to construct paragraphs that follow the cumulative pattern—they articulate the most important thought in a topic

---

EXERCISE 2.2

Ask students to look at a writing exercise or essay they've written, and to mark the most important sentence in each paragraph. Ask them to look for places where that sentence might be better placed either at the beginning or end of the paragraph, and to think about why. Then ask them questions to help them reflect on the patterns they see: Are you a cumulative or a periodic thinker? What effect does it have when the controlling sentence, with the most important information and thinking, comes at the beginning of a paragraph? At the end?

---

sentence at the beginning of the paragraph, and add and modify in the following sentences. But a quick glance through any anthology of professional essays reveals a problem, for professional essayists tend to write *their* paragraphs in the periodic style, *leading up* to the most important thought in their paragraphs in their final sentences. They do this because their ideas are often so complex or counterintuitive that they could not be understood without the train of thought and pieces of evidence that precede them.

In actuality, students need to be trained to write *both* kinds of paragraphs, since each serves an important rhetorical purpose. Moreover, some professors will want topic sentences to organize students' papers, and some will expect the kind of thinking that can only be done in periodic paragraphs. Marking these forms as the class progresses through its anthology of readings can help students to see what is happening in their own paragraphs. This work of pointing and naming can provide students with a vital basis for experimentation. We should direct students to examine their writing too, in light of this practice, as we do in Exercise 2.2.

Like paragraphs, essays can be understood as organized by cumulative and periodic patterns, and bound by coordinate and subordinate modification. The thesis/supporting point essay in Figure 2.1 follows a cumulative pattern with coordinate modification; if the "base clause," or main thought, is articulated in the first paragraph, then each supporting point refers back to, or modifies, that initial base clause without necessarily relating to or modifying the supporting point immediately preceding it. We draw a diagram like Figure 2.1 on the board to represent this for students, with rectangles standing for each paragraph in the five-paragraph essay, and arrows standing for the movement of ideas.

Note the way this essay structure turns the entire essay back, in the end, to repeat what has been said in the beginning. Its entire movement is inward, avoiding anything that would trouble the truth of the initial thought. Its shape is one that masquerades as "absolute" knowledge—communicating a singular idea, which the rest of the essay attempts to clarify, exemplify, and argue. If we ask students to write in subordinate cumulative and periodic structures, however, they must find relationships between each of their subordinate ideas, and construct a more complex pattern of subordination with more nuanced connections. A periodic essay structure using subordinate modification—in other words, in which each paragraph

Figure 2.1. Structure of the Thesis/Supporting Point Essay

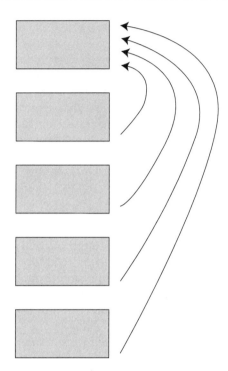

builds on the idea in the paragraph before it—can be conceptualized on the board in a figure like the one in Figure 2.2. In this essay formation, the first idea is clarified, charged, reset, and fashioned anew with each subsequent paragraph.

Figure 2.2 represents only a first step toward generating complexity. The periodic pattern with subordinate modification begins to describe the form most often used by exploratory essayists such as Virginia Woolf, George Orwell, Alice Walker, and many others, in which the idea reached at the end is a long way from the idea with which the writer began, but is still tightly bound, through a complex connective process, to that initial thought. But if you look more deeply into great essays, you'll see even more complicated subrelationships; you'll see thought circling backward, returning to concepts that haven't been mentioned for pages, suddenly revealing the form of an idea of a breadth and significance it never could have possessed without such a movement.

Below, we provide an exercise that can help students begin the process of learning cumulative and periodic structure, and explore the relationship between sentence structures that generate thinking and the larger structures of thought that form their paragraphs and essays.

Declarative, cumulative, periodic, and chiasmatic sentences all generate ways of thinking and teach patterns of organization, as do other forms of sentences that employ balanced or serial parallelism. The teacher need not be an expert in grammatical form to do this work, for we can learn alongside our students. It isn't

Figure 2.2. Structure of the Periodic Essay with Subordinate Modification

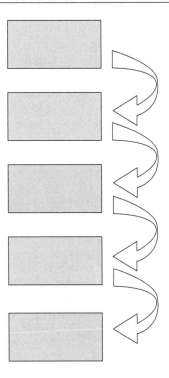

even absolutely necessary that we call these forms by their right names (although it doesn't hurt), so long as we call them by a name that makes sense and helps the class remember their shapes and the kinds of thinking they enable. After all, our ultimate goal is to help students write better, not pass a class in taxonomy. Rather, teaching form rigorously means maintaining an open mind, paying attention to the shapes in which our students think, and helping them find new shapes that challenge their habits of mind and help them construct beautiful sentences and essays.

EXERCISE 2.3

Ask students to look at a writing exercise or essay they've written and mark the most important sentence in each paragraph. Does the most important sentence in the essay come in the first or last paragraph of the essay? Is that where it should be? Have them look at the other sentences—in what direction does the modification of their ideas flow? Can they draw a diagram of this pattern of modification and development, to make it work better?

USING PARALLELISM TO GENERATE MULTIPLE INTERPRETATIONS

We don't have the space to explore many more sentence structures here, but let's consider parallelism for a moment. Parallelism works by repeating and changing syntactical gestures for rhetorical effect. In parallelism something must stay the same and something else change, if only slightly. Because of this, parallelism can lead writers to make fine distinctions, and to proliferate new modes of description. In a student essay entitled, "Martyr: Cassie Bernall and *She Said Yes*," Kerri Hunt employs parallelism and parataxis (the juxtaposition of clauses or images without connectives) to give a quick progression of interpretations of one phenomenon:

> Two troubled teenagers at Columbine killed "Cassie," the human being, for her "Yes." But Cassie, the person, died when the story of her "Yes" reached an America waiting, eager to make meaning of a terrible tragedy. And it was that second martyrdom, a martyrdom of abstraction, which killed her more completely than any bullet could. Cassie has been mythologized; she has been canonized; she has been commodified.

Kerri uses parallelism in this last sentence to condense into one location in her essay the three ideas that provide its structure. This excerpt is from a final draft, but as the following exercise shows, we also can work backwards, with the help of parallel sentence structures, to get students to make the multiple interpretations that working with parallelism can demand, and then work outward toward essay structure.

CULTIVATING CONSCIOUS MIMESIS

Once we have established sentence, paragraph, and essay structures as a primary mode of thinking in the class, our classroom environment will naturally

---

EXERCISE 2.4

Ask students to choose a central piece of evidence, a phenomenon that they know they want to write about in an upcoming essay. Have them put that phenomenon in the beginning of a propositional sentence, for example, "Reality TV is." Then have them write as many incarnations of that sentence as they can in five minutes, trying each time to provide a new interpretation of the phenomenon rather than simply provide a longer description of it. To generate economy of expression, ask students to limit their interpretations to less than five new words each time. When the time is up, ask them to choose the three sentences that are most different from one another—that, although true, create tension among them—and combine them into one parallel sentence through parataxis (repeated semicolons). Hear some of these sentences aloud. Do they suggest a structure for the ideas of a section of the student's essay?

work to help students grow comfortable working with the rhetorically crafted sentences of professional writers. We call this work *mimesis*, loosely defining this term as a learning through imitation. When students take part in mimesis, they don't imitate in order to copy the ideas or language of professional writers. They consciously aim to augment the form of their own thinking. A mode that occurs almost unconsciously for writers ensconced in effective written language, mimesis helps students' thinking to grow more complex as an organic result of the new forms in which they find themselves writing.

To see the effect of this work in action, consider the way one student, Colin Forbes, summarizes and extrapolates on the ideas of theorist Mark Taylor (1999) in a series of graceful sentences:

> Economy will become so abstracted, so symbolic, that "means and ends are internally related in such a way that they are mutually constitutive" (Taylor 164). Capitalism will exist to perpetuate capitalism; money will exist so that money can continue to exist. People will spend money to make money, and make it to spend it, money becoming then the embodiment of ideology, no longer a tool but an independent force. In that mankind lives so that they might serve it and serves it so that they might live, "money is God in more than a trivial sense" (158).

Note that Colin has used sentence forms that reflect the ideas he's reading in Taylor; since he's writing about circularity and inversion, he embodies these in his sentence structure. He is using forms that Taylor tends to use, because he has immersed himself in that text, along with parallel, chiasmic structures, because he has been reading Marx, and cumulative structures because we studied them in class. This is mimesis at work—but it is a conscious mimesis, one that puts Colin in charge of his essay's ideas.

PEDAGOGICAL STRATEGIES FOR THE CLASSROOM

If we get students to articulate what limits them as writers early in our time together, their fear of writing ungrammatical sentences will probably come up repeatedly, enough to create a sense of (potentially productive) crisis in the classroom. As teachers, we should communicate our desire to help our students learn the forms of beautiful (and correct) language at exactly the moment when they communicate this fear, and in those terms. Confidence is the clearest and simplest reason—for students, the most accessible *motivation*—for becoming conscious of the way language works, and self-conscious of one's own language in the best way.

There are other, more important reasons, which render confidence only an effect of this course of study in the end. But the grammar/syntax issue is one in which what the teacher needs to know is different than what the students need to know, at least in the beginning. Discussing the form/content unity we unpacked early in this chapter would be overwhelming for students; letting them know they can only improve their thinking in writing if they expand their syntactical options would intimidate them; and talking about this early on would waste time because they will learn it best by doing it. Teachers, then, need to generate their own understanding about what sentences have to do with thinking, in order to be on the lookout for the most opportune moments to draw students' attention to the relationship as it surfaces in the professional texts they read, and in their own writing.

We hope by now that you are eager to start drawing your students' attention to the sentences they write, and pushing them to add more shapes to their repertoire alongside your work on content in the classroom. What follows is a meditation on some of the practices we employ in the classroom to set up such a process; the stamp of your individuality will undoubtedly be different than ours, but by sharing these we hope to emphasize the care that needs to be taken in integrating technique instruction into the whole performance, and the whole community, of the classroom.

One method for preparing oneself for "opportune moments" in the writing process is to create a running list of sentence patterns you would like students to learn as you begin a semester. With a list in hand, you'll be ready to draw attention to them as they come up. Be prepared, too, for students to discover patterns on their own that they want to imitate, that you name together as a class.

At the beginning of the semester, have students draw attention to powerful sentences in what you read together. When you've focused on a particular sentence, ask students for verbs describing the kind of thinking that sentence does. For example, if you're looking at a periodic sentence, students might say that it is delaying, building up to a thought, building suspense. Teach the form of the sentence so that they can see that a sentence in this structure will usually do these thinking actions, and then ask them to use a periodic sentence in their next writing assignment. When you've seen the assignments, you can discuss the nuances of constructing the sentence based on the successes and failures you see in their writing—perhaps by compiling a list of some of their periodic sentences into a handout and looking at them as a class. In this way, the knowledge about these forms of thinking is generated communally, with you as a kind of knowledgeable scribe.

As you accumulate a common language about sentence structures, and a collection of sentence types you've been working on as a class, you can compile handouts listing the types you've learned, with memorable examples from the professional texts you're reading and from student papers. You should also ask students to play with grammatical structures throughout the semester, and keep asking. When it comes time for them to write their major essays in the class, ask them to use a certain number of the sentence types they've learned.

As students' consciousness of complex forms is increased, and as they develop language for naming the shapes they see in sentences and paragraphs, their ability to wrap their mind around the whole of each piece of writing they do will increase as well. In the next chapter, we explore the way this logic of working dialectically between standard forms and the writer's own thoughts can help him or her to conceptualize a whole train of thought that moves powerfully from one idea to the next in the academic essay.

3 *Making Thinking Move*

> For philosophical problems arise when language goes on holiday.
> —Ludwig Wittgenstein

Thinking always happens in one form or another. Even freewriting, such as the writing about a personal problem we asked students to do in Chapter 1, takes on particular shapes. The problem we continually face as teachers is that language seems to break down when it comes time to describe and evaluate these thinking patterns in our students' exercises and essays. In the midst of grading 50 papers, we fill the margins of their papers with vague words such as "doesn't flow," "clarify," "more analysis needed here," "connection?" and "transition?" But how much do these words actually help students learn? The problem, from the student's point of view, is that achieving something like "flow" ends up amounting to a guessing game; even if they can say of others' writing that it "flows" or "doesn't flow," they have trouble seeing it in their own and knowing how to "fix it."

For teachers, the problem is largely one of time. We write these vague words because to comment on the particular problem in each place where a student's essay doesn't flow takes more time and energy than we have to give. Too often, we end up doing this work in individual conferences with students, leading them by the hand through revising steps they can't figure out on their own. But teaching the shape of essayistic thinking on an individual basis is not only time-consuming. It leads students to become too dependent on us. We must find effective ways of teaching students to learn to do this work on their own, if they are going to be able to carry the tools they acquire in our classes into their academic writing across the disciplines.

WORKING WITH THINKING MOVES

In this chapter, we suggest a set of strategies for getting beyond "flow"—for articulating what coherence, transitions, and analysis look like rhetorically, in such a way that students can learn to perform them on their own. This training is based on three underlying assumptions:

1. Students learn better writing through the act of mimesis; we can speed up this process through a collaborative naming of forms and structures.
2. Thinking in more rigorous ways and shaping beautiful essays are best conceptualized as parts of the same project; we should simultaneously teach students

to employ forms that encourage thinking, and thinking that necessitates beautiful forms.

3. Classroom work should be devoted to training students to train themselves so that they can carry such work out of the classroom into their thinking lives.

As we saw in the last chapter, the thesis/supporting point essay form can limit students' ability to develop their ideas. Because of this, the writing teacher should challenge this form now, so that students can reimagine how to work within it later. When we talk with our students about challenging this form in our classes, we remind the class of the forms of cumulative and periodic essays (described in Chapter 2) and ask if students can name the difference between the thesis diagram, in which all the thinking arrows point back toward the beginning claim, because each successive paragraph is designed to support that claim, and the periodic diagram, in which each paragraph builds on the next. Students can see that in the periodic essay form, the thinking is moving forward; ideas grow, accumulate, are questioned, and are continually revised throughout the essay's trajectory. We will begin the journey toward writing this kind of essay by asking students to study the ways in which professional writers move their ideas forward. Because this is more difficult for them to see, we introduce the concept of "thinking moves."

The internal structure of advanced essays, both familiar and academic, can be characterized as a progression of ideas, introduced and interwoven as the essay progresses. These introductions and interweavings consist of a number of turning points, surprises, twists—moments when the essay's established thinking is added to, revised, called into question, problemetized, or transcended in some way. When professional writers make these turns, they do so with rhetorical emphasis, by shaping sentences and paragraphs that are designed to frame the turn in a rhetorically powerful way, so that it is clear to the reader not only that the writer's thinking is *moving*, but that it is moving in a particular, intended direction. Turns in thinking, and the rhetorical shapes that house them, though distinguishable from one another, occur simultaneously. They organize the essay, guiding readers through a careful choreography that displays each new idea as flowing from those that have come before. We call this double motion, this intersection of powerful thinking and rhetoric, a *thinking move*.

Over the course of a semester, we develop a repertoire of thinking moves together with our students. This work begins by directing our classes to find and name them in the professional essays we read together as a class. Once students have gotten the hang of identifying them, we begin to require that students organize their essay drafts by their own thinking moves. In other words, rather than ordering their thoughts according to their evidence, which is the default mode— examples in support of a claim—we ask students to organize their evidence by clearly articulated modifications or expansions of their thinking.

Given how central our work with thinking moves is in our classrooms, we take care to introduce it to our students in a compelling way. One way that's proven successful is showing the ending of Quentin Tarantino's (1994) film *Pulp Fiction*. Because our students' essays tend to work within a triangle of written evidence, evidence from personal experience, and their own reflections, this is a great film to use—its ending employs all those elements. In the final scene of the film, Samuel L. Jackson's character, Jules, has a written text he's trying to understand (a Bible verse about vengeance that he recites aloud each time he kills someone), a personal experience that is changing the way he thinks about that text (earlier in the day, bullets passed through him and at his partner Vincent Vega, played by John Travolta, without injuring them), and some reflections about the state of his life and his career as a hit man. His final thoughts make important moves within this triangle and comment profoundly on the film's story lines.

The final scene is set in a diner. Jules and Vega are eating breakfast at the end of a long day of crime when a pair of robbers, Pumpkin and Honey Bunny, hold up the diner. Jules and Vega attempt to get control of the situation, and when Jules's final monologue begins, Jules holds a gun to Pumpkin's head, Honey Bunny's sights are set on Jules's head, and Vega's sights are set on Honey Bunny.

By showing this final scene to our students, we present them with a dilemma that is allegorical of their process as writers—we might interpret it, with our students, as the filmic equivalent to the kind of thinking problems our students may be working with in their essays. Jules transcends the dilemma by giving Pumpkin the $1,500 that's in his wallet, and then by delivering a speech that brings an end to the problematic situation and to the film. In the speech, Jules quotes his text and articulates the interpretive problem he's been wrestling with, and then shares three possible answers:

> You read the Bible? There's a passage I got memorized, Ezekiel 25:17 . . . "The path of the righteous man is beset on all sides by the inequities of the selfish and the tyranny of evil men. Blessed is he, who, in the name of charity and good will, shepherds the weak through the valley of the darkness. For he is truly his brother's keeper and the finder of lost children . . . And I will strike down upon thee with great vengeance and furious anger those who attempt to poison and destroy my brothers. And you will know I am the Lord when I lay my vengeance upon you" . . . Now, I been sayin' that shit for years. And if you ever heard it, it meant your ass. I never really questioned what it meant. I thought it was just a cold-blooded thing to say to a mother-fucker 'fore you popped a cap in his ass. But I saw some shit this mornin' made me think twice . . .
>
> Now, I'm thinkin', it could mean you're the evil man. And I'm the righteous man. And Mister .45 here, he's the shepherd protecting my righteous ass in the valley of darkness.
>
> Or, it could be you're the righteous man and I'm the shepherd and It's the world that's evil and selfish. I'd like that.
>
> But that shit ain't the truth. The truth is: you're the weak. And I'm the tyranny of evil men. But I'm tryin', Ringo. I'm tryin' real hard to be the shepherd.

By establishing two alternative readings of the Bible verse and transcending these with a third, Jules performs the movement in his thinking rhetorically. Jules's initial interpretation is that he's righteous, and the man at the other end of his gun is evil, and the gun is the shepherd. The second, the alternative, inverts the first and adds: perhaps Pumpkin is righteous, Jules is the shepherd, and the evil is outside both of them, in the world somewhere. That's the interpretation Jules would like. But because it's not true, because the truth is more complicated than that, he must move to the "transcendent" position, offering an interpretation of the Bible verse that suggests that Pumpkin is neither righteous nor evil but weak, and that Jules himself represents the "tyranny of evil men." Importantly, Jules concludes that he occupies two contradictory positions at once: he is an evil man also striving to be a protector, a shepherd. This last interpretation simultaneously synthesizes elements of the previous two interpretations (evil is inside men, not outside in the world somewhere) and makes a move toward personal responsibility, for he understands that he can strive against it. It is because he makes a move along not one but both of the triangles in Figure 3.1 that his final realization in the film is so satisfying.

A discussion of this scene, then, leads us to consider a set of thinking moves we might call "dialectics." Thinking dialectically means challenging each thesis with an antithesis and then moving toward a synthesis between the two poles, but it also means occupying multiple perspectives simultaneously as a writer. The *Pulp Fiction* example is particularly useful because it shows a dialectical movement not only on the level of propositions, but in terms of the speaker's position as well. It is because Jules implicates himself in this dilemma, articulating his position as more complicated than he would like it to be, that this dialectical move carries special weight. Ask the right questions and students will be able to figure this out, through discussion; they will also see that the thinking moves Jules employs are important in structuring the film—because he makes both these moves, a satisfying ending is created.

Consider how Savannah Shange, whose thinking problem concerning hip-hop we quoted in Chapter 1, makes a dialectical move by calling her initial idea into question. As we saw, Savannah's initial thinking problem concerned the fact that the authenticity of hip-hop is lost through commodification. Here she questions whether hip-hop music ever existed as a pristine, authentic aesthetic movement in the first place:

> At the same time, as much as I fantasize about hip-hop's fabled past, the legitimacy of my argument is slippery. Is it possible to distill the essence of an inherently hybrid form? If the foundation of hip-hop is the sample, that means the music is always co-authored by both the "original" artist and the innovator . . . [Celebrating hip-hop] is a strange dance between defying tropes of unitary identities and origins, on the one hand, and at the same time reinforcing the binaries of real/not real, us/them, self/other.

In the dialectical move above, Savannah has opposed and critiqued her initial idea, that something essential in hip-hop culture was being lost through its com-

Figure 3.1. The *Pulp Fiction* Example

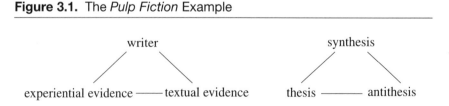

modification; here, she counters that description by claiming the form itself is a hybrid, never essential. And she's begun the process of doing the thinking that takes both realities into account—describing a dynamic of negotiation between resisting appropriation, on the one hand, and avoiding claims of unitary identity, on the other.

Dialectical moves function like the cumulative and periodic structures we studied in the last chapter, providing a step toward complicating thesis-centered writing. Students must master dialectical thinking moves to become skilled writers. But this is only a next step. It should be noted that dialectics are not the last stage in the process of essay writing, for they are still a form driven by direct statements, by proposals and refutations, by oppositions. We believe that students should also be urged to play outside this frame of writing: to seek, identify, and use a wide variety of thinking moves. The particular set of moves we teach in each class varies each semester, because to work well the study of these moves must grow out of the particular texts our classes are reading. Our aim isn't to give students a list of moves and simply make them do them; we want to find and name the moves together, so that they are intertwined with the content and vocabulary of our classes.

There are, however, a few foundational kinds of thinking moves—some dialectical and some that transcend dialectics—that we teach again and again, because they are so helpful for beginning writers. In what follows, we share some of these favorite moves, discuss their importance for beginning writers, and share some examples of students employing these moves to organize their essays and lend motion and emphasis to their thinking.

READING THE LEVELS

We call the first category of thinking move "reading the levels"; the core of the move is to show how one's thinking progresses beyond a too-simple or untenable interpretation. What students don't understand intuitively is the potential rhetorical power of "showing their work" as their thinking progresses, by framing their multiple interpretations as different levels at which a given text or phenomenon is operating. In practice, this framing work helps the reader along by explicitly marking an essay's movement from one way of understanding an issue to another.

Reading the levels helps students in a second way as well, for by asking students to explicitly construct these moves, we help them to see that thinking is actually taking place at the moment when they feel most stuck. In their minds, they feel stuck when they haven't yet found an authoritative conclusion—but reading the levels teaches them to exploit this lack of authority, and the incremental process of finding a better way of thinking through their problem, to show movement of thought in their essays.

One way to get this thinking started is to ask students to call a first-level, conventional, official, or otherwise too-easy reading into question by providing their own second-level, more rigorous interpretation. In an excerpt from the student essay provided below, you will likely feel the phrase "But it's not that simple" lurking beneath Lina Wells's text:

> However, the most interesting aspect of Catherine's character is not that she alters her behavior to suit others. After all, that characteristic is precisely what Berger claims is universal in women. What is interesting about Catherine is that she is able to make her presence constitute not only what others can do to her, but also what she can do to others; this lends Catherine a characteristic that Berger claims as "male."

Here's another of Lina's level-reading moves taken from the beginning of a research paper on *The Great Gatsby*, for a literature class. Note how reading the levels serves to undercut several popular misconceptions of the 1920s that have deep political ramifications, setting up a rich problem for her essay:

> The 1920's remains one of the most romanticized decades in American history. It has become "a blur, a kind of montage of gangsters terrorizing great cities and heedless flappers dancing the Charleston upon the tabletops of speakeasies about to be raided by lively but ineffective cops. . . ." Yet the popular image of the twenties is something of a myth, that eclipses the central conservative forces of the times: censorship in various forms, the Ku Klux Klan, and most important to this discussion, limited views of female sexuality.

Later in the paper, Lina will show how *The Great Gatsby* embodies these multiple levels, its superficial liberalism thereby concealing a deep critique of liberal culture. She will further problematize this reading of the novel by exploring the ways in which Daisy and Jordan represent conflicting ideals of feminine sexuality that cause "tension between women and men and within women themselves" in the novel.

Finally, in Sarah Dell-Arto's essay on fashion and suffering, consider how she refuses the alternative theories that suffering is just a step on the way to beauty, our ultimate goal, on the one hand, or that we, on the other hand, love suffering for the sake of suffering, and construct our beauty standards in order to do so. She is in favor of a third alternative that is a bit more complicated:

> Usually, we assume that we search for pleasure and strive to avoid pain. But the history of the fashion and beauty industries makes it obvious that we are always searching for both—that part of the pleasure we seek is pain itself. And perhaps there's something even more complicated going on here. When I wear heels to a club, perhaps I am touting my glory as a female—I can do it all, and I can do it in heels . . . perhaps it's about proving to ourselves that we can accomplish things most men couldn't handle—bikini waxes, bras, facial scrubs, stilettos. In a bizarre female version of machismo, we must find as much satisfaction in seeking pain as we do in seeking pleasure. The pain shows our ability to endure and serves as a reminder that in today's society, we often have to work twice as hard to get equal results. And we do, and there is satisfaction in the fact that we do.

In this thinking move that sets up the end of her essay, Sarah transcends the double binds of pleasure and pain, performed femininity and performed masculinity. At the same time, she makes a move back to the personal, to the part of all this that matters to her, and is able to construct a new way of understanding the problem, made possible by the care she took in showing her work along the way.

EITHER/OR

Students can thwart the urge to jump to an easy claim by setting up two possible interpretations, in an either/or formulation, to be transcended later. This variant of the dialectical move, which we also sometimes call refusing the double bind, is a hallmark of the writing of Slavoj Zizek, a writer we often use to teach thinking moves because he makes them so explicitly.* Here is an example of Zizek (1995) refusing the either/or, or double bind, in an essay that discusses the way we interpret traumatic images:

> From the traditional perspective, the [wreck of the] Titanic is a nostalgic monument of a bygone era of gallantry lost in today's world of vulgarity; from the leftist viewpoint, it is a story about the impotence of an ossified class society. But these are commonplaces that could be found in any report on the Titanic—we can easily explain, in this way, the metaphorical over-determination which confers on the Titanic its symbolic weight. The problem is that this is not all . . . By looking at the wreck we gain an insight into the forbidden domain, into a space that should be left unseen . . . This terrifying impact has nothing to do with meaning. (p. 27)

Here, Zizek refuses the two alternative ways of interpreting images of the wreck, and by shifting the fundamental questions we should ask about the things that traumatize us, Zizek carves a space for his own thinking to take shape. By taking the time to offer us the views that he wants to set aside, Zizek has marked his awareness of the controversy in a way that lends importance to his very different interpretation of the matter.

In the following example, Elizabeth Moore sets up an either/or interpretive problem in the beginning of her essay on James Joyce and Roddy Doyle:

> Still, the question of aesthetics arises. Which is the greater contribution to Ireland: a work that speaks directly to the Irish people, or a work that sacrifices popular appeal for critical acclaim? Joyce and Doyle had very different relationships to the same country . . .

Later on, Elizabeth rejects both sides of the either/or, arguing that Joyce's work is, "in a more complex and difficult way, as pro-Irish as Doyle's":

> Though [both Doyle and Joyce] are associated with distinctly separate classes and eras, both are pro-Irish and in their literary contributions we can see the

---

*Our work with "reading the levels" and our engagement with Slavoj Zizek derives from a long and fruitful collaboration with Ben Stewart, whose research in psychoanalysis and writing has deeply influenced our thinking in the classroom and throughout this chapter.

emergence of a different voice—a voice that transcends the typical perceptions of Irish literature as either sentimental or thoughtlessly nationalistic.

By focusing on both authors' work with language, Elizabeth rejects the double bind, the clear-cut alternatives, in favor of a third option.

INVERSION AND CONTRADICTION

Our students' texts, like all writing, will always be haunted by paradoxes and contradictions. Often, sections of student essays that seem plagued by the absence of thought, or by confused thought, are the way they are because the writer is (consciously or unconsciously) attempting to ignore, avoid, or cover over a paradox or contradiction they've encountered in the process of their thinking. When we ask students to begin to question their too-simple claims and thesis, and to think in dialectical ways, contradictions will increase in their writing. This is a good thing, for it lays claim to why we need revision, so that complex and sound ideas can develop over several drafts. Rather than criticize students for not making sense, our job as teachers is to gently point out the contradictions they're falling into, and ask them to state their contradictory ideas about the problem explicitly, as a thinking move.

At times like these, when students begin to generate claims that emerge out of dialectical thinking, their thinking can begin to take the shape of *inversions*. When this is the case, we can encourage students to work with chiasmic sentence shapes (discussed in Chapter 2) to bring those claims together. Candy Goh, for example, was writing an essay in which she alternated between arguing that pop culture's influence on us is always bad, because we lose ourselves in the search to become like our idols, and arguing that we stand to gain from imitating our pop cultural icons. We asked her to bring those two claims together in a chiasmic form, and doing so helped her to develop her idea further. Candy writes:

> Perhaps participating in popular culture is not necessarily as detrimental as it first seemed, as it is in the process of mimicking that we lose ourselves, and it is only through this loss of self that we can gain self-identity.

In this case, the inversion of the first idea led to a paradoxical truth—Candy uses it near the end of her essay to resolve her competing claims.

On other occasions, competing claims can provide a tension that calls out for thinking (rather than, as in the above example, a satisfied resolution of a problem). In this case, they should be framed explicitly as *contradictions*. Notice the way that Mike Dyaduk outlines a series of contradictions, employed humorously in a *Saturday Night Live* sketch, to elucidate a thinking problem about the contradictions the Internet embodies:

> *Saturday Night Live* sometimes parodies this trend in television news reportage in a skit in which the hosts' faces can't even be seen behind the dozens of "informative" displays on the screen. This creates two contradictions: first, this overabundance of information, ostensibly meant to facilitate our access to information, in fact makes that process all but impossible. Second, and more

importantly, the human part of the equation—the exchange of information between the program's hosts and its viewers—has been literally eclipsed by technology not unlike that employed by the Internet, in this case resulting in chaos.

The contradictory nature of the "information revolution" brought about by the Internet provides the locus for Mike's thinking throughout this academic essay. Such work offers a second example of a contradiction that is located outside the writer, who identifies and analyzes it. But writers also discover contradictions within their own lives, in which case the contradiction can be framed as a dilemma, as Elaine Sanchez does in the following excerpt:

> Hence, the dilemma. Though to the computer I'm one hundred percent Filipino, to my kin, I'm an alleged foreign copout—a white wannabe. Therein lies the illegibility of being two things at once.

Elaine frames this contradiction to establish the main problem of her essay. As a personal dilemma it has to be tied to the larger problem of illegibility to provide a rich problem for her essay.

So when writers use contradiction, or show tension between two competing claims or truths, it can be for the sake of transcending them—to move beyond the conflict these thinking moves set up. But sometimes recognizing the contradiction is the whole truth—and that truth becomes a discovery that may itself provide a new problem. Once students have seen the ways in which writers use paradox and contradiction in the professional texts they read, we can begin to ask them to systematically draw out the hidden paradoxes in the texts and cultural productions they analyze, as well as in their own ideas.

DRAWING THE LINE

When we involve students in problem-centered writing, they will begin to find that thinking problems tend to generate more thinking problems, and that the contradictions and dialectics they explore will always lead to more of the same. In the face of this endlessly spiraling process of rereading and rethinking, students need strategies for stopping, for making claims, and for taking a stand. The crucial move that writers must be able to make is that of distinguishing between what is trivial and what is truly problematic—and ideally, they must be able to take a stand on what can be thought or done about that delimited problem. The thinking move that can help them here is one we call "drawing the line," and it's particularly useful for ending an essay that has been exploring a thinking problem. Beginning her essay with personal experience of the hostile factions that developed at an exclusive women's college she attended, Clare Fitzgerald sets up a thinking problem about the "destructive nature of exclusionary behavior," taking up a range of evidence to figure out whether groups can provide belonging without excluding. In the end, she decides that they cannot—and that this is an eternal, universal problem that will never be totally figured out. But she doesn't stop there—she reframes the problem to show where she draws the line:

It is not that I do not understand that divisions between people are part of life, or that I don't believe that they are often important and can be necessary to leverage power and make change. I accept that binary oppositions serve as a major way to categorize people and that they are deeply ingrained in our society. My concern arises when we invest more value in them than they deserve. When we begin to value our membership in groups over the attributes and actions of the individual, the group can gain a momentum that easily leads to negative consequences, for as one surrenders part of themselves to the greater group, they also relinquish much of their responsibility.

Drawing the line can happen just about anywhere in an essay, of course, but it's a good suggestion to give students when they're floundering, perhaps for the first time in their academic lives, for a way to write a conclusion to an essay about an overwhelming theoretical problem.

WEAVING

So how can students bring it all together? Of course, an essay is not simply a random collection of thinking moves. Shifts of mind within an essay must build on one another, providing an overarching trajectory, a train of thought. Practice in building individual thinking moves does help students learn to see forms, and this practice on the local scale—the sentence and the paragraph—does help students to be able to identify, and imagine, the form of an entire essay. But students also need concrete techniques to bind these individual moves together, as well as the multiple pieces of evidence they will use in their essays—written texts, personal experience, visual evidence, or accounts of scenes or events, whatever they're working with. In our classes, we initially encourage students to bring in as many pieces, and kinds, of evidence as they can connect together—the more surprising the connections, the better. Encouraging students to overwhelm themselves with phenomena they are analyzing gives them a crash course in learning to find surprising new connections and ideas. But they need concrete strategies for building connections in a way that will bind such a complex collection of evidence and ideas together.

Central among our strategies for teaching students to build connections across the course of an essay, in order to lend it form and a sense of progress, is the technique of weaving. An essay by Alex Obercian, included at the end of Chapter 8, is exemplary of this work; each time Alex brings in a new piece of evidence, he reflects back on at least one and often several of the pieces of evidence he's thought about so far. And when he weaves back, building connections, new ideas result. For example, Alex's essay begins with the Columbine shootings and the controversy over the Christian right's attempt to get copies of the Ten Commandments posted in schools to prevent such violence. When he moves on to talk about a Christian product, Shoes of the Fisherman sandals, he weaves back to mention the Ten Commandments and, out of the meeting of the two pieces of evidence, develops a new idea:

An appealing ocean-teal color and, by all accounts on the manufacturer's website, of sturdy construction, these sandals would appear normal enough. However, the soles are alternately etched with the words "Jesus" and "Loves You," the idea being that a stroll on the beach will leave imprints in the sand that will likewise imprint any wayward soul who should happen to gaze upon these divine footprints.

To wear these sandals, or to display the Ten Commandments in school, is to believe that spirituality can be imparted instantly, that the power of the Word is so overwhelming that merely seeing it can lead to inspiration, or even salvation.

Here is a straightforward use of weaving to return to earlier evidence; it establishes a thinking pattern that will become more and more complex over the course of Alex's essay, as he returns to evidence and ideas to construct an innovative theory about the sacrificiality of certain magical attitudes toward language. It is this weaving that provides his essay with both its movement forward and its organization.

OVERVIEW

As is evident in the progressions you will find in the last three chapters of this book, we encourage students to practice thinking moves in ways that will lend coherent form to their essays by requiring that they make a certain number of thinking moves in each exercise and draft. These numbers are part of a game—a set of limitations that creates a space in which students can innovate. The idea is to foster abundance: We don't take the specific numbers themselves too seriously. We use them to suggest to students that they can speed up their thinking process in a way that simultaneously helps them to build coherent and powerful form into their writing. If students set out to weave back to earlier evidence and/or ideas at least ten times in their essay, for example, they are bound to find new connections between pieces of evidence and parts of their thinking. In this way working within formal restraints reveals new content—and students have practiced strategies that will help them to be able to develop their thinking outside the boundaries of our classrooms.

4 *Working with Written Evidence*

> Always now this work of construction and deconstruction—letting no thing
> simply "be"—seeing everything instead as a product, as the fruit of some
> labour, some desire, some ideology.
>
> —Tim Etchells, *Certain Fragments*

Whether our students are writing personal or academic essays, we always require
them to work with written texts as evidence. By the time they leave our classes,
we want them to be able to read and incorporate these texts in several ways: to
provide information and strengthen claims, to borrow and develop the theoretical frameworks and ideas of others, and to challenge, question, and deconstruct
professional writing in order to develop new ideas of their own. Though these
skills will help our students in other college classrooms, our reasons for teaching
them reflect a deeper belief as well: our students cannot become wise and mature writers until they allow generous and rigorous reading to transform their
thinking.

The kind of reading that leads to good text incorporation, and the kinds of
text incorporation skills that encourage good reading, are difficult to define and to
teach. Often teachers resort to the language of "conversation" in order to explain
this dynamic, asking students' ideas and the ideas they glean from texts to "speak"
to each other. But what does this mean? As a provisional definition, we suggest
that good reading and text incorporation consist in creating reciprocal, recursive,
and dialectical relationships between the thinking of the writer and that which is
found in the written source. Moreover, though the ideas our students generate
through such interpretive work should transcend the thinking done within those
sources, they should never leave that thinking behind, but return to it throughout
the course of an essay.

So far, we have discussed work with written texts mainly in terms of mimesis; we've shown how we lead students to identify and imitate the sentence structures, paragraph and essay shapes, and thinking moves that professional writers
employ. This pedagogy lays the foundation for working with written evidence,
because it teaches students to do three things: first, to identify the choices a writer
makes as she puts her texts together; second, to investigate the relationships between form and meaning that are crucial to doing close readings; and third, to
imitate the kinds of dialectical thinking moves that will be essential to incorporating written texts. Here we continue this work by analyzing those beliefs about
written texts that limit students' reading and writing, and providing exercises for
building essays through rigorous reading.

WHAT STUDENTS BELIEVE ABOUT WRITTEN TEXTS

Let's take a look at a couple of typical examples of text incorporation from early in the first semester. When asked to create a conversation between their own ideas and the ideas of others, student writers often default to one of two modes represented by these examples. The first student offers this reading of Jamaica Kincaid's essay "On Seeing England for the First Time":

> Jamaica Kincaid (2000) writes that the "space between the idea and the reality is wide and deep and dark." She is surprised that the reality of England is different from her idea of it, as a colonial subject. When I first saw the reality of college, I experienced the same thing.

Another student attempts to make use of Baudrillard:

> What the beautiful people don't necessarily realize about the lower class is just how important it is to their own gilded aristocratic existence. As Baudrillard (1981) writes, "culture . . . is nothing but the phantom support for the operation of the medium itself, whose function is always to induce mass, to produce a homogenous human and mental flux" (p. 67). Social classes exist to maintain their existence. The upper class, being in a position of power, wants to persist.

In the first example, the student subsumes her experience and thinking under the umbrella of the idea provided by Kincaid; in the second, the student ignores the complex meaning of Baudrillard's quotation in order to use it to support her thinking. We can characterize these two common modes of incorporation as "sacrificial readings," modes of interpretation that forefront one kind of thinking at the expense of another:

1. In the first, students sacrifice their own thinking in favor of repeating the ideas of the writer(s) they read and quote, failing to either challenge or build upon them.
2. In the second, students sacrifice the texts they read and incorporate in favor of their own ideas, using their chosen thinker's words only as proof, failing to attend to the context from which the words are taken and the complexity of the ideas they express.

The pervasiveness of these two kinds of sacrificial readings (found in student and professional writings alike) suggests that the ability to read well and incorporate texts skillfully does not arise *naturally*, thanks to greater knowledge and experience on the part of our students. Students need to be taught to perform interpretive work so that it can become a catalyst for sharpening their own new ideas and deepening their reading of texts. But training them to do this takes time and care.

To teach these skills, we need to identify the assumptions and beliefs that lead students to sacrificial readings. In both of the modes illustrated above, students treat quotes as seamless blocks of meaning that self-evidentially articulate the same thing as what the student is saying. They believe in the wholeness of the text and the unity of its meaning. But these examples also demonstrate a contra-dictory belief: that texts are made up of pieces, extractable quotes, that can be used without regard to the whole text.

Both of these beliefs have kernels of truth in them. Reading and text incor-poration must be attentive to both the whole text and its fragmentary, porous nature. In fact, it is in this dialectical position between taking texts apart and put-ting them back together that we want to locate students from the start of their reading, until they ultimately incorporate texts into the finished work of their essays.

What follows are a series of strategies for leading students into this dialec-tical relationship with texts, and teaching them to perform it well.

A PARADIGM FOR PLAYING WITH WRITTEN TEXTS

In his book *Certain Fragments*, performer and writer Tim Etchells (1999) cele-brates the pleasure of playing in construction sites and ruins. This celebration elu-cidates a belief underlying the performances of Etchells's theatre group Forced Entertainment: places, texts, ideas—everything human beings have made is incom-plete, and in everything there are traces of a process of construction. For Etchells, viewing the world in this way opens up a space for creativity, pleasure, and the best kind of vandalism. This kind of play in incomplete places serves Etchells as a metaphor for his group's philosophy of performance. It also serves us as a meta-phor for the kind of reading we train our students to do:

> We always loved the incomplete—from the building site to the demolition site, from the building that was used once and is no longer to the building that will be used . . . The fascination of ruined places, of incomplete places. It seems unethical to admit—the strange charge of buildings left to run down—but they always were the best places to play—stinking of previous use, ready for transgression. Every piss you took in the corner and every window you broke and every game you played in the old factory, the old house was a writing over its everyday . . . And do you remember burying things in the foundations of new houses as they were being made? What a surprise for somebody—these traces of some inexplicable ritual? Always now this work of construction and deconstruction—letting no thing sim-ply "be"—seeing everything instead as a product, as the fruit of some labour, some desire, some ideology. (p. 78)

When we teach Etchells's essay, students gravitate toward this passage—every-one knows the pleasure of playing in places that feel haunted or are not yet fin-ished. The notion of playing in a ruin or construction site provides a good metaphor for the experience of working with a written text, for it is the ability to see a text as "a product, as the fruit of some labour, some desire, some ideology" that provides entry into thinking. To view the texts we read as traces of a process, as products constructed through choices. To look for the assumptions buried in the foundations of texts, and find the traces of the rituals through which the writer has made his ideas so sacred, so beyond questioning.

When students practice this kind of reading, they are less inclined to take a professional writer's words as a given, or a truth to be dispensed; instead they can

analyze words as symptoms of deeper structures. These deep structures then become the student's chosen object of analysis. The slow, deep reading entailed by
this process of taking a text apart in turn helps students attend to the whole text
when they contextualize the quotes they excerpt for incorporation.

THEORETICAL FRAMEWORKS FOR TEXT INCORPORATION

The first steps toward accomplishing these goals in the classroom lie in convincing students that pieces of writing do not spring full-blown out of a writer's
head. Since all texts are products of a long and often unfinished process, they should
not only be examined in terms of what they mean, but also in terms of how they
were made. This thinking forms the foundation of reading well. We can teach students two closely related theoretical frameworks for working with written texts
that give them a sense of what it feels like to read a text well. The first framework
might be called "psychoanalytic," and the second, "deconstructive." In class, we
will name these theoretical frameworks explicitly in the classroom (this can be done
with or without giving them Freud, Lacan, or Derrida to read), because students
will have more confidence in these unfamiliar reading methods when they know
that they are widely practiced in the university that surrounds them.

The central psychoanalytic beliefs that we teach are that written texts, like
people, have an unconscious; that for this reason they often say more than they
intend to, if we read them closely; and that texts, like dreams, harbor much of their
meaning in their structure. The central deconstructive belief that we teach is that
texts organize themselves through secret assumptions that often come in twos,
binary oppositions that may be more or less hidden in the text, but that keep its
logic from falling apart.

Students process and analyze both modes of reading best by employing
them, so we give them a set of questions that can be asked of any text. As a class,
we apply these questions to a short text like the one included below, taken from
Bill McKibben's (2003) essay "The Posthuman Condition":

> The past five hundred years have elevated us to the status of individuals, and re-
> duced us to the status of individuals. At the end of the process, that's what we are—
> empowered, enabled, isolated, disconnected individuals. Call it blessing or call it
> curse or call it both, that's where we find ourselves . . . The great danger, in other
> words, of the world that we have built is that it leaves us vulnerable to meaning-
> lessness—to a world where consumption is all that happens, because there's noth-
> ing else left that means anything . . . And the only real resource that many of us
> have against that meaninglessness, now that the church and the village and the
> family and even the natural world can't provide us with as much context as before,
> is our individual selves. We have to, somehow, produce all that context for our-
> selves; that's what a modern life is about . . .
>
> But now *we stand on the edge of disappearing even as individuals.* Most of the
> backdrops have long since been dragged off the stage, and most of the other actors
> have mostly vanished; each of us is giving out existential monologue, trying to make
> it count for something. But in the wings the genetic engineers stand poised to slip
> us off the stage as well, and in so doing to bring down the curtain on the entire
> show. (p. 16, emphasis in original)

After having students read the excerpt, we distribute a list of questions inspired by psychoanalytic and deconstructive theory. Below are the questions, and examples of the kinds of answers we might hear in discussion when these questions are applied to McKibben's text.

Psychoanalytic Questions

> What do you think this writer wants most in the world?
> What does the form of the text contribute to the intended meaning?
> Where is the form in tension with the intended meaning?
> What possibilities are foreclosed by the text?

Deconstructive Questions

> What concepts are equated or identified with one another?
> What binary oppositions structure this writer's assumptions about the world?
> Of these binary oppositions, which terms are valued?

How can we respond to the psychoanalytic questions at the level of content? When modeling such work for our students, we can begin by thinking about the way an author manages two terms: desire and fear. On the surface, we might say that McKibben desires *meaning* most of all, but we might read below the surface and find another desire—for at the same time, McKibben also seems afraid of how fast the world is changing.

On the formal level, psychoanalytic readings look for tensions and contradictions, too—only in this case, they are sought in terms of the text's structure. Here, McKibben's essay creates ambiguities and contradictions by means of lists and an employment of parallelism. For example, he uses phrases such as, "elevated us to the status of individuals, and reduced us to the status of individuals," "empowered, enabled, isolated, disconnected," "Call it blessing or call it curse." These formal tensions emphasize the difficulty of finding meaning in the modern world. But they might also inadvertently highlight McKibben's own ambivalence about the status of the "individual," and raise the possibility that there might be different ways of thinking and feeling about both our individuality and its potential disappearance.

As we continue on with the psychoanalytic questions, we might find that McKibben forecloses a number of possibilities, most significantly the possibility that many of the problems he finds in contemporary life have existed throughout human history. He ignores the possibility that there may not be such a clear line between being engineered and not engineered, and that there may not be such a rigid distinction between being an individual and being a member of a community. And he ignores the possibility that our lives now might provide us with "context," even if it is of a different sort than that experienced in the past. The central question for this psychoanalytic framework reads: What is McKibben trying to avoid by writing off these possibilities?

Next, we direct the class to consider deconstructive concerns, exposing how a text comes to say what it wants to say. Closely tied to psychoanalytic readings of textual structure, deconstructive interpretations provide more methods for foregrounding what an author wants to avoid, and analyzing how a text's attempts to claim something are frustrated by its own form. By teaching our students to look at which terms are treated as allies and which as opposites, we give them straightforward tools for reading any text deeply.

When we apply the deconstructive questions to this excerpt, we might find that McKibben equates meaning with context, and context with the church, the village, the family, and the natural world, while he opposes consumption to meaning, present to past, culture to nature, and the individual to the group. Under this deconstructive reading, if these terms fail to constitute genuine opposites, McKibben's logic—and his text as a whole—begins to fall apart.

In class, when we perform this exercise of related interpretive methods, we ask our students to imagine what questions this exercise raises and what new ideas it might lead them toward. Once we identify deep structures in a piece of writing, we begin to open up a space for thinking about the text. Whether they agree or disagree with McKibben about the apocalyptic nature of genetic engineering, opening up his logic, speculating about his desires, and looking for relationships between form and content will have led students into deep and concentrated reading, that in turn may provoke new ideas of their own.

TEXT INCORPORATION AND WORKING WITH LANGUAGE

While cultivating these modes of reading provides entry into developing ideas about texts, students still need practice in treating texts as nonunitary—as construction sites that can be played with—in order to be able to carry out skillful text incorporation. They also need strategies for remaining affective to the whole texts, even as they excerpt quotes for focused analysis. Teaching students concrete strategies for text incorporation works similarly to teaching them thinking moves— they need to study the forms of these moves in other texts, name them for themselves, and practice imitating them. In the following section, we provide some examples of a few text-incorporation thinking moves that we want each student to be able to make, and share classroom exercises that train students to make these moves in their writing.

Borrowing a Theoretical Framework

When students use the theoretical framework of another thinker, it is crucial that they incorporate it into their thinking, introducing quotes that help them summarize the framework by weaving the thinker's language and their own together. Notice the way that Akiemi Glenn, whose essay we include in full in Chapter 7, subtly and gradually builds up to incorporating René Girard's theory on sacrifice into her account of her personal experience, borrowing the clarity of his framework even while she maintains her authority in her own text. She does this by setting his language up within her own story:

Death was a fact of farm life . . . My family's survival, in the cultural sense, stipulated that there be ritual killings every November so that we would not forget the hardships of our forebears . . . The [sacrificial] victims were always animals, but they were always our animals, the livestock kept in pens, hand fed and named. Enough like us to matter, to be cared for, and enough like us to suffice for us in the symbolic death. According to the anthropologist Rene Girard (1977), this kind of sacrifice does more than express gratitude externally, from humans toward nature. It also serves to ritualize and structure societal violence, the kind of violence that might erupt from interpersonal tensions but is channeled into communal, ritual action. For sacrifice "from the animal realm" we choose victims "who were, if we might use the phrase, most human in nature," writes Girard in *Violence and the Sacred*. An animal victim is sought "at the crucial moment to prevent violence from attaining its designated victim" (p. 6).

In this example, Akiemi's consistent formal use of Girard allows her to vivify her own story with the force of a theoretical interpretation from beginning to end. Rather than simply point to a passage that grants her work a hint of authority, the entire texture of her piece testifies to the influence Girard had in the process of her creation.

Students can be led to practice the reading and thinking work that prefigures such work on incorporation in the classroom exercise we provide in Exercise 4.1.

Dialectical Text Incorporation

The most basic move in working with theoretical texts, the dialectical move, is to both agree and disagree with the writer—to show what the theory helps to explain, but then to be able to move beyond it by showing where it falls short, as Sarah Dell-Arto does in this excerpt:

So [the social critic Malcolm] Gladwell can probably explain how stilettos became popular or if corsets are going to make a comeback any time soon. But he seems to have glossed over the big picture—that is, he can see the individual trends themselves, but not the connections between them. He

---

EXERCISE 4.1

On a day when students have brought their theorists' texts to class, have them circle the ten most important words—for their purposes—in the essay, chapter, or excerpt. Have them write these words at the top of a sheet of paper, and then reconstruct the theorists' ideas without looking at the text, incorporating those ten words, but avoiding any theoretical phrases. When students are done, ask them to return to the text—what did they leave out as a result of writing in their own language? How can they add in this supplemental information? How might they apply this version of the thinker's theory to an idea in their own writing?

cannot account for the primacy, among practices that become "cool" or even are considered necessary, of practices that take time and sacrifice: the gym body, the uncomfortable clothing, the diet-thin body, the complete lack of wrinkles. Gladwell can never really get to the root of that problem, because it can't be tracked as a single trend. It has been happening in culture for thousands of years—corsets, bound feet, porcelain skin, lip disks, stilettos. We like to separate ourselves from the people who wore corsets and bound their children's feet. We like to think of ourselves as more humane and more progressive. But in such a progressive society, we still torture ourselves in the quest to achieve beauty—and perhaps it is our need for that torture that motivates the trends, more than it is the trends that motivate our need for torture.

Once writers begin to think dialectically, with and against the texts they read, they naturally move toward transcending the text's parameters, leaping off into their own ideas; Sarah's chiasmic distinction, in the last line, is categorically different than Gladwell's theories about trends, but she couldn't have gotten to it without thinking with and against him. To encourage students to do this kind of productive dialectical work, we ask students to create what we call "dialectical notebooks," as shown in Exercise 4.2.

This exercise doesn't always provide students with the particular content of the dialectical moves they will make vis-à-vis their written source in their final essays. But even when it doesn't, it helps them feel the structure of dialectical work, and teaches them that over the course of working with their sources they must ask again and again what is the same and what is different between their ideas and those of their sources, and be willing to change their interpretation until they develop the best one. When they incorporate their quotes, they should stage this dialectical move in the reading of the quote, articulating what they agree with and then moving clearly, with the help of words like "but," "on the other hand," and "however," toward disagreement.

EXERCISE 4.2

Ask students to draw three lines down a piece of paper, forming four columns. Then they should choose the most important quote, for their purposes, from the written text they're working with. Have them write it in the left column, and then fill the second column with their reflections on it—a summary of their interpretation of the quote's implications for their own ideas and topic. Ask them to pass the page to a classmate, who will fill the third column with questions that call into doubt the connections the first student is drawing— this student is responsible for determining how the professional writer's and the student's ideas differ and even come into conflict. When the page is returned, they should fill the fourth column with new thinking about the source text that accommodates the questions that have been raised.

Surprising Connections

If the last move we taught was about finding important differences between the student writer's ideas and those she is quoting and incorporating, this one is about finding surprising similarities. We ask our students to make surprising, rather than obvious, connections among written texts, telling them that important thinking also happens through connecting what doesn't seem, on the surface, to be connected. We encourage students to look for unlikely ways of connecting written texts to their own ideas, and while sometimes these connections will fail or feel forced, more often than not students will discover interesting new insights through this work.

In the following excerpt from his essay on Internet culture, quoted in the last chapter, Mike Dyaduk uses Roland Barthes's ideas about being in movie theaters, glossing them with his own experience, to reveal a paradox about the Internet:

> I have often wondered what draws me and so many others to the movies. I tend to go almost every week, usually catching the bargain matinee show each Friday. But the cheap price is hardly the main attraction. I am drawn by the possibilities intrinsic in every movie—for what is a movie if not a channel for the interaction of human ideas. The images are there in front of you, and the theatre is filled with dozens of people each sharing in your experience; yet the dim lighting shrouds each observer in darkness, separating you from the others and creating a somewhat false sense of seclusion. Roland Barthes (1994) describes this experience in a piece titled "Leaving the Movie Theatre," in which he observes that "the darkness of the theater is prefigured by the 'twilight reverie' . . . burying [you] in a dim, anonymous, indifferent cube" (p. 419). This concept of privacy created within a public space resembles the foundation of the Internet, where each user enjoys a sense of remoteness in what is perhaps the largest, most interconnected public domain we have seen thus far.

Rather than connecting his idea to that of a writer who talks about isolation on the internet, Dyaduk connects it to an idea about another medium altogether—and because he's chosen well, this comparison opens up a space for him to do thinking and connecting work.

Finding surprising connections should begin early in the essay-writing stage, while students are choosing which outside written sources they want to work with. Although they have to do that work on their own, we can train them to believe in the possibility and importance of surprising connections through classroom work. We do so through a practice of bringing these connections into classroom discussion, often through focused free writing. As often as possible, when we're discussing a reading, we have students take a few moments to write about phenomena that are similar in form to one the writer's describing, but different in content.

From Form to Content

If there are kinds of reading that lead to good text incorporation, there are also kinds of text incorporation that lead to good reading. Until now, we've been readying students by teaching them new reading and thinking skills; now we're going to teach the text incorporation rules and skills that, in turn, send them back to their written sources to do even better reading.

Once students have grown accustomed to reiterating a thinker's ideas in their own words, and practiced making dialectical moves toward articulating important differences and surprising similarities, they can begin the work of text incorporation. Every composition handbook supplies rules for such work, but while teachers always have students purchase handbooks and ask them to refer to these guides, we haven't seen evidence that looking at handbooks helps students incorporate other writers' ideas into their essays in graceful and smart ways. What does work is to build on the philosophy behind our work with sentences by teaching our students to require certain forms of themselves.

We establish three text incorporation rules for students, each implying a rigorous attention to the *form* of the incorporation, and developing out of the kinds of reading we've been teaching students to do:

1. When you extract a quote from the rest of the text, you cannot let its words stand on its own; you must characterize the kind of thinking that the source writer is doing.
2. You must treat each quote as needing interpretation; rather than assuming it has one clear meaning, you must take it apart and read it for us in your essay.
3. You must connect each quote to other parts of the text from which it's taken, and return to the ideas in the quote at least one more time in your essay.

In establishing these rules, we place formal restrictions on the student that require her to create new content in response to the quotes she's using, and the rigor of the restrictions encourages that content to take the form of thinking. We'll conclude with two exercises that get students to play with these rules in a way that generates good interpretive work, new thinking, and new ideas at the same time as it helps them to fulfill the conventions of quote incorporation for academic writing in the humanities.

EXERCISE 4.3

Give students a long list of verbs gathered from instances of quote incorporation in professional essays. These are verbs that writers have used in signal phrases introducing quotes. Ask students to think about a writer whose ideas they are incorporating into their essay, read the list, and choose five verbs that seem to characterize a kind of thinking their writer is doing in his essay. Then ask them to write a sentence or two around each verb; without quoting the text, their job is to put the verb into a statement about what the writer's doing and support it. If their writer is "nurturing," for example, they'll be responsible for saying what he's nurturing, why, and how. Below is a shortened version of the verb list we give.*

---

*This list and exercise were given to us by Sally Stratakis-Allen, whose research into and ideas about teaching text incorporation have influenced our work in the classroom and in this chapter.

List for Exercise 4.3

Announces	Entangles	Labors	Obscures	Repudiates
Asserts	Fabricates	Lambastes	Offers	Retaliates
Answers	Foreshadows	Lavishes	Overlooks	Revokes
Argues	Foretells	Learns	Overreacts	Savors
Bemoans	Generates	Longs	Perverts	Sentimentalizes
Brags	Grapples	Magnifies	Preempts	Surpasses
Circles	Gushes	Maligns	Ponders	Sympathizes
Chastises	Hammers	Masks	Postures	Testifies
Contemplates	Hopes	Minimizes	Preaches	Transcends
Deliberates	Immortalizes	Misappropriates	Rambles	Valorizes
Denies	Impoverishes	Moralizes	Reconciles	Warns
Denounces	Impugns	Negates	Reinforces	Withholds
Discloses	Jests	Nurtures	Reminisces	Witnesses

Once students have written these sentences, we hear some of them and discuss where they might go in relation to a quote being incorporated. Some sentences will sound more like introduction, and some will sound like reflection after the fact; in discussing which is which, we begin to develop strategies for what kind of thinking needs to be done around a quotation.

We encourage students to use these sentences around quotes, and to use active verbs such as these in their signal phrases (rather than "she writes," "she states," etc.). In much the same way that teaching sentence structures encourages students to develop the context of their thinking, the formal restraint of requiring them to employ active verbs returns them to the texts they're quoting, to develop deeper readings. The exercise that follows is designed to direct students to be recursive in their thinking about a quotation, and to be attentive to the whole text as they incorporate it. It provides a final stage in moving students toward effective use of professional texts in their writing.

EXERCISE 4.4

Have students take an important passage from a professional text they're working with, photocopy it, and then cut it into three or four sections, each one with its own idea. Ask them to choose the section that seems most provocative to them and incorporate it into a paragraph in which they read and interpret it, using it to develop ideas of their own. Then instruct them to return to the other fragments and decide what their new ideas have to do with the thinker's other ideas. Have students revise and expand their paragraph, relating the thinking they've already done to the parts of the passage they didn't initially focus on.

IMPLICATIONS

Throughout this chapter, we've shared methods for encouraging students to do reading and text incorporation that is dialectical, recursive, and reciprocal. Learning to do this means learning to avoid sacrifice, whether that's the sacrifice of the student writer's ideas, the ideas in the written evidence, the context from which a quote is taken, or the new possibilities the quote excludes. And it means coming to believe that written texts are always products of labor, and that this fact opens up a world of potential ways of reading. As students become more and more familiar with the way that they can look for patterns that indicate the deeper structures of texts they're reading, the structures of their own writing and thinking can become more and more apparent to them. This ability to see forms is crucial to thinking in general—as we argue throughout this book—but it is a matter of particular urgency when students are required to revise their own essays, both in our classes and beyond. In the next chapter, we build on this training in reading written texts for the thinking patterns they reveal, as we share concrete exercises for teaching students how to revise.

5 *From Thinking to Knowing*

> By recognizing our uncanny strangeness we shall neither suffer from it nor enjoy it from the outside. The foreigner is within me, hence we are all foreigners. If I am a foreigner, there are no foreigners.
> —Julia Kristeva, *Strangers to Ourselves*

To write is to extend words over a void, when we do not yet understand our thinking.

The work suggested by this book aims, in part, to teach writers to embrace this void, rather than hide from it: To write well, we've argued, we must be willing to delay decisions about what our ideas are for a while, until we've discovered the best form for those ideas. We've shown how revealing and studying forms, particularly those of essays, sentences, thinking moves, and written evidence, can support this process of lingering in uncertainty. But in the end, when we put our writing out into the world, when we turn it in for a class, we need to know something, and be "certain" about it. We need to know enough to find the best words, so that our readers will know what we're talking about. And we want to accommodate the expectations of the audience we are writing for, and the conventions of the situation in which we are writing.

Even so, no matter how well we understand these conventions, once we have written our first drafts, we revise, just as we write, over a void, because our readers are not with us. Impossibly, we must put ourselves in their place—imagining what they need to know, in what order, and how they would best be moved through the twists and turns of our thought. The void over which we revise lies between what we are trying to express and what the reader might think we mean. Good revision means filling in this gap in knowledge between writer and reader by ascertaining when enough has been written so that most readers will understand—when the thinking moves have been clearly articulated and sufficiently sustained, gaps filled, repetition eliminated.

Students are often uncomfortable with the provisional certainty that revising demands of their writing, and the abyss over which it must be done. They frequently ask us how they can know for certain when it's time to stop writing and revising, and when they need to do more. This problem is connected to the difficulty of seeing their writing objectively: "I can see what's wrong with other people's writing, but not my own." Once they have written something down on paper, our students tend to treat that thinking as somehow solid and immutable (in much the same way that they treat the texts they read, as we saw in Chapter 4), even if they feel strongly that it's lacking. In order to revise, to chisel away at the thinking they've set in stone, students need distance. Here we might borrow and modify the language of Julia Kristeva: In order to revise effectively, students need to become strangers to their own writing. If we ask our students to rework their essays before they are able to see their own thoughts as if they are those of a "foreigner," they invariably undertake the project of revision as one of "fixing" those grammatical and argumentative problems that are readily identifiable as errors. But a little revision isn't always a good thing.

This limiting conception of revision as "fixing" is critiqued frequently in composition handbooks, when their writers urge students to treat revision as a thorough process of rethinking, restructuring, and rewriting. Programs for "writing across the curriculum" are founded on the assumption that requiring multiple drafts, supported by peer and teacher feedback, will improve student writing across the board. But even though everyone on the teaching side agrees that revision is essential to the process of writing, it remains one of the most difficult things to actually teach in the classroom. Without an overarching methodology that shifts students' understanding of how writing works, one or two peer editing sessions won't necessarily save a struggling essay. And even in writing workshops that dedicate themselves to revision, getting students to deeply rethink and revise is quite a challenge. Add to that the importance of getting students to leave our classrooms with the ability to revise essays and papers to perfection in a range of academic situations, and teaching revision becomes a particularly pressing and troubling challenge for the writing teacher.

And yet it is through absence—through finding good ways to remove ourselves from the students' process—that the problem must be solved. What students need, in order to be able to revise, is to become that person most foreign to their conceptions of themselves as writers: a teacher. To take our place they need to have solid principles in mind for how good writing works, so that they can interact with their own drafts as if the writing had been done by someone else. As the semester progresses, then, and particularly as it draws to a close, teaching our students to revise means revealing the structures of our pedagogy itself. Once through the essay-writing process with us a time or two, our students have enough knowledge and experience to see the patterns in their approaches to writing. Most importantly, they can begin to name these patterns in their own words. When students can say what they know about essay structure, for example, in concrete, detailed, strategic ways—and in this way move from thinking to knowing—they can become strangers to their writing, and therefore teachers to themselves. The forms to be revealed in this work, then, are those of the class itself.

In the following sections, we begin with strategies for helping students to work with revising the essays they write in our classes, and move on to share exercises for leading students to be conscious of the structures of our teaching methods. Our hope is that they will choose those they would like to make their own as they move into the rest of the university.

TEACHING STUDENTS TO BEGIN WITH A DIAGNOSIS

What makes teaching the process of revision difficult—at least in the abstract—is the obvious fact that most revision is "site-specific." Although student papers often share certain common problems (a love affair with generalizations, improper citations, awkward transitions, and so on), it is also true that the revision work one student draft needs might backfire on another.

How can we help students figure out what kind of revision they need to do on a given essay? It may seem counterintuitive, given our emphasis on process, but we've found that students need to grow alienated from their work, if only for a bit, in order to figure out what revising to do next. Though usually used in a pejorative sense, we needn't fear the word "alienation" here, for it is this alienation, this distance from one's own text, that is crucial for students to attain if they are to become their own teachers. Our goal should be to facilitate a dialectical movement between process and product, where the work that students do in the process stage and the product stage each informs the other. While the *process* stage aims to draw students closer to their work (until they believe in their own projects), the *product* stage of the dialectic requires students to distance (or alienate) themselves from their essays so that they can critique them (and thereby make their essays, in the end, even more their own).

So how do we show students how to treat their essays as finished products? There's no transporting them between psychic states, unfortunately. In order to become alienated from their writing, students will need to manage a framework of goals and objectives that helps their writing become strange to them in the process of revising their essays. At the same time, these goals and objectives must be flexible enough to apply to a wide range of styles and formal shapes, for we don't want to merely supplant the old five-paragraph essay formula with a new one.

In order to train our students to recognize the goals that we've been working on, and name writing qualities and strategies for themselves, we develop checklists together with our students, usually in the class period before the one when the rough draft is due. We ask them to name what we've been working toward, and as they articulate what they understand, we write the goals on the board. After class, we type these goals up in the form of a checklist, and when they come to class with their rough drafts, we break them up into small groups and hand the checklist out as a workshopping guide.

Though in our classes each checklist is developed with a particular essay in mind, below we provide a generalized checklist that articulates the overarching goals of the class. Because it's generalized, you'll see that this checklist is far too long to actually use in one workshop; we share it with you here to provide a sense of the way we formulate questions that reflect the work and vocabulary of the class. By making shorter, more focused lists with our classes, we can train students to translate complex classroom work into concrete, identifiable goals—a skill that will help them discover what to work toward in other, future writing contexts. As the semester progresses, we will ask students to continue to hone their skills with checklists in small groups, emphasizing that the goal of these small-group exercises is to become capable of reading one's own work independently—an ability that's developed by becoming a good reader of others' writing.

Revision Checklist

1. Does the writer have a clearly articulated problem? Is it complex and compelling? Does the problem avoid obvious and/or unanswerable questions, or

ones that would have to be answered with masses of factual information, establishing instead tensions and dilemmas that will be thought about in the essay?

2. Does the writer have a main idea about that problem?
3. List pieces of evidence here:
4. Does each piece of evidence allow the writer to develop new thinking about the problem?
5. Has the writer written these reflections in his or her essay in a way that shows both what's new in their thinking after each piece of evidence, and how that new thinking is connected to earlier thinking in their essay?
6. Does the writer weave back to mention earlier pieces of evidence, even as he or she introduces new pieces? How many times? Can he or she do it more?
7. How many thinking moves does the writer use? Is the overall structure of the essay organized according to thinking moves, rather than according to evidence? Is it clear in the transitional sentences that the writer is moving from evidence to evidence with thinking moves, rather than with language that makes it sound as if he or she is listing examples?
8. Does the essay's ending make a move toward thesis, antithesis, or synthesis (whichever comes next) at the same time as it makes a move toward taking a stand on a new way of understanding the thinking problem?
9. Are the sentence structures powerful and varied? Has the writer worked to develop sentences that push his or her thinking beyond the obvious?
10. Is the essay's language precise, its punctuation correct, and its syntax clear and beautiful?
11. Is the essay titled in a way that captures the essence of the idea, as well as the reader's attention?
12. Does the essay employ proper citation and documentation conventions, and include a "works cited" page?

In the checklist above, the criteria move from early stages in the essay-perfecting process to more developed ones. The first few questions function as a litmus test for deep and substantial revision—if students find these questions unanswered in their drafts, this should indicate that much work lies at the level of discovery and expansion. If students don't get stuck until the last few questions, the set of tasks will swing toward augmenting the ideas that already exist in their papers, revising for surface issues. This continuum of criteria can be helpful in teaching students to diagnose their stage in the revising process. Diagnostic stages can be defined in the following way:

1. *Revising for Discovery*: mining what is already there for new ideas, then searching out new evidence and developing new thinking.
2. *Revising for Expansion*: filling in gaps, building transitions, practicing weaving, developing argumentation, reordering, and refining sentences and methods.
3. *Revising to Polish*: clarifying awkward moments in argumentation, syntax, and tone, and cutting excess and repetition.

When we give students these structures for diagnosing the stages of their classmates' essays and their own work, they take important steps toward knowing when they are finished writing and when they need to press forward.

REVISING FOR DISCOVERY

Let's think through this first category by reading some excerpts of a student essay. In the following passage, Sidra Qazi's ideas are only beginning to be fleshed out, and the writing at this point is only a stepping stone to thinking:

> The subject, History, has been taught in school systems for as long as people have been around. For ages our ancestors have documented the events in their lives, and we have incessantly been forced to imprint them into our memories. The Egyptians built the pyramids, the Romans conquered lands, and Columbus discovered America. The History of the Universe has become a subject all too familiar to many.
>
> At times it seems as though that there is no use in reading about the lives of our ancestors, and the disasters that occurred during their times. If we are raised to learn from our mistakes, why does it seem that history has been doing the exact opposite? We have continually been repeating our mistakes and seem to be learning very little from them. Why is it so hard to learn from the mistakes of the past?

In this excerpt from her first draft, Sidra is beginning to ask questions, which is good. She is in search of a thinking problem that can create the matrix for her essay. Several telltale signs should help Sidra and her classmates identify this draft as one in need of revising for discovery:

1. The thinking problem is not yet clear.
2. Generalizations appear out of nowhere, before evidence has been given.
3. There is no specific evidence given that helps us to understand her initial questions or their importance.
4. Her crucial term, history, is scapegoated for the dynamic she wants to critique.
5. There is an unexamined contradiction that is not stated as such: We believe we should learn from our mistakes, but history does the exact opposite. In this contradiction, not yet formulated clearly, there is slippage between "we" and "history," which indicates that she has not yet decided on what phenomena, and what particular dynamics, mark places or moments where this "not learning from mistakes" happens. The passive voice indicates that there is a problem of responsibility that she's not discussing yet.
6. That is, she is not implicated, not evidentially involved, in the problem she's outlining, which is always evidence of a gap in thinking.
7. Her paragraphs are short and her sentences short and repetitive.

Each of these indicators points to the fact that there is discovery work that needs to be done—it's not time to clean up her language, but for Sidra and her peers to circle the most important and problematic words and phrases in her essay (words and phrases such as "incessantly" and "continually" and "History of the Universe"), begin raising questions about them, freewrite about these questions to develop conceptual frameworks in which to consider her evidence, and perhaps go out in search of new evidence that can help her to draw out her thinking, rather than generalizing first and proving later.

Students can train themselves to diagnose this first stage only when they work collaboratively with readers who are willing to tell them they're not yet in the final stages of essay writing; though it can be hard to do this for oneself, the most important element in learning to do so is developing a careful attention to the requirements of the assignment. In the writing class in which Sidra wrote this draft, the essay prompt asked writers to draw claims out of evidence, develop a clear and thorough thinking problem in the beginning of their essays, avoid facile generalizations, and search out important cultural contradictions that can be stated clearly and explicitly. Because these requirements were laid out, peer editors asked Sidra to look in her essay for these elements; because she found so few of them, Sidra knew that her essay was in need of rethinking. Consider Sidra's new beginning, after "revising to discover" what she really wanted to ask:

> In his new film, *One Hour Photo*, Robin Williams describes the art of picture taking. We choose to only document the happy times in our lives. We always take pictures of our celebrations: our weddings, birthdays, graduations. We never choose to document the times in our lives when we have been met with strife and discord. These times are hidden away, but by hiding the stories of our lives, we are choosing to hide our history. We mask the important things that must be documented in our lives in order for our descendants to learn from our mistakes. We mask these secrets with monuments, ceremonies, and memorials, and try to give these tragic events a concrete explanation. Through these explanations we lose the harsh reality of the event, and thus we find ourselves documenting watered down emotions rather than the true feelings of pain and torture that have been felt . . .

By choosing a cultural object that provides her with a springboard into the issues on which she wants to focus, moving to implicate herself in the problem she's outlining, and outlining the problem in a clear set of tensions between what "we" believe and what we do, Sidra has done a fine job of focusing her thinking and building a more effective essay beginning. Now she is in a position to revise for expansion—to show how she thinks *One Hour Photo* gives rise to the notion that though we shrink from documenting trauma, it is part of our duty to confront and represent the facts of our lives in their harsh truth. She is ready to build relationships between these thoughts through sentence combining, and to organize these sentences into thinking moves that build on one another.

In Exercise 5.1, we provide an example that can motivate "revising for discovery" in the classroom.

REVISING FOR EXPANSION

When students have learned to organize their writing through thinking problems, work with evidence, and develop ideas, they are ready to expand their

EXERCISE 5.1

Ask students to choose two pages of an exercise or draft they've brought to class—pages that feel particularly undeveloped to them, but promising. Ask them to read the two pages to two or three other students. The listeners' job is to think about the excerpt through the lens of the following five questions:

1. Is there a clearly articulated thinking problem?
2. Does the problem move beyond obvious and/or unanswerable questions to establish tensions and contradictions that can be thought about?
3. Is it developed with the help of specific, concrete, compelling evidence?
4. Is the writer implicated in the problem?
5. Is there a clear and complex idea being developed in response to that problem?

If one or more of these questions can be answered in the negative, the essay clearly occupies the "revising for discovery" stage. Wherever the listeners find a lack, they should help the writer think of strategies for rewriting the work. For the next class, ask students to write a completely new version of the two pages they brought to class, accommodating the issues raised by their readers, without borrowing the structure or any of the sentences of the first version.

---

ideas, lingering in the details that matter and showing the steps of their thinking in the gaps still present between sentences, paragraphs, and essay parts. Let's look at an initial version of the beginning of an essay by another student, Natalie Torresy:

> Basketball icon Allen Iverson is quoted to have said, "Tell [the public] not to believe what they read or hear [about me]. Tell them to read my body. I wear my story every day, man." To note, Iverson was talking about his tattoos, but to what extent are our lives revealed on our skin, on our bodies? As individuals we are confined to our minds, analyzing and scrutinizing ourselves internally, yet as social beings, we can only access another's body, and vice versa. It is therefore vital for us to be aware of the "story" we portray through our bodies.

In this case, we must decide just how we can ask Natalie to push her work further. When students can feel a rich problem developing already in a paragraph, commenting on the writer's draft may mean merely circling important words and drawing arrows between them. They can ask, in this case, how readers are supposed to understand the relations among the key words—tattoos, minds, bodies, and stories—in this excerpt. In fact, this very question led peer editors to suggest that Natalie add more steps between thoughts, for they felt these steps were necessary in order for her point to become effective. This challenge brought her to the following revision, in which she takes more time to build the problem:

Philadelphia 76ers point-guard Allen Iverson is quoted as having said, "Tell [the public] not to believe what they read or hear [about me]. Tell them to read my body. I wear my story every day, man." To note, he was talking about his tattoos, but to what extent are our lives revealed on our skin; on our bodies? As individuals we are confined to our minds, analyzing and scrutinizing ourselves internally, yet as social beings, we can only access another's body, and vice versa. It is impossible to enter the mind of a peer, assessing their thoughts, morals, or values, yet we are members of a society based on physicality, visual images, and snap judgments. As Elizabeth Lozano (2000) notes, because "[the body] is an expressive and sensual region open to the scrutiny, discipline, and sanction of the community", it is vital for us to determine just what "story" we portray—and what story is depicted or interpreted—through our bodies (p. 231). Understanding this double movement suggests that bodies often act as channels with which we voluntarily frame our lives—and in which our lives are undoubtedly framed.

Unlike Sidra, Natalie was able to work within the basic structure she had already laid down, filling in gaps by adding evidence and new thinking. Once this expan-

---

EXERCISE 5.2

Upon bringing their first drafts to the class, ask students to break into small groups and pass their essays to one another. They'll read these drafts through the lens of the following questions:

1. Does the writer develop a new idea about the thinking problem each time a new piece of evidence is introduced? Students should mark new ideas, as well as places where new ideas need to be developed, because there's new evidence, but are not.
2. Does the writer weave back to mention earlier pieces of evidence, and earlier ideas, even as he brings up new ones? Students should mark all the places where the writer does weave back, as well as three to five places where he or she doesn't but should.
3. How many thinking moves does the writer use? Is the overall structure of the essay organized according to thinking moves, rather than according to evidence? Students should mark each place where the essay is organized well by a strong thinking move, and each place where a thinking move feels necessary but is absent.

After such a thorough reading, it's a good idea to give students time in class to do some writing in response to the gaps in thinking, evidence, and essay structure that have been marked. They'll use this work to guide them as they write another, more complete draft that they'll turn in to us or bring to us in conference.

sion occurred, Natalie was ready to revise for polishing—to work on word choice and phrasing, to find the most perfect words for these ideas.

Using Natalie's paragraph as a microcosm of the larger issue of revising for expansion, we can imagine how a workshop might direct students toward helping one another's essays improve (see Exercise 5.2).

REVISING TO POLISH

Once students have allowed for problems, ideas, and arguments to fully develop in their writing and added the language necessary to guide the reader through their thinking, they are ready to begin the process of polishing. This means removing the excess: cleaning up confusing language, tangled claims, and unnecessary flourishes. It means touching up sections that still present gaps in the structure of the essay. In other words, after our students have written essays that lead the reader through a series of dynamic linguistic and thematic moves, it is time to give the reader the final gift of elegance and clarity of expression.

Colin Forbes's essay "Consuming God" offers an example of a draft ready for such polishing. We'll look at a section midway through the essay, and then make concrete the revising strategies we suggest for polishing work:

> In the 1970's a group of "artists" known as "punks" attempted to challenge and shatter the manner of thinking which allows such a society to exist. As they used them, symbols were not cohesive; they refused to amount to the same thing, unified under a single god-like abstract. They offered no alternative to life as we know it, but in the very least hoped to end the process by which image upon image synthesized "reality." Essentially, where capitalism assembled symbols to stand for something unified and true in money, the existence of relative value, punks assembled the same symbols only to negate all of them and destroy. They created a theoretical and ideological void.
>
> To observe footage of Johnny Rotten and the Sex Pistols on stage or in interviews at any time during the years 1976 or '77 is to witness a paradox, a staunch refusal to stand for anything at all, yet standing hard nonetheless. His career as a punk was a well-planned and perfectly executed exercise in contradiction, absolutely nothing at all. He was a parody of the society that produced him, its harbinger of doom, and yet also a member of it. In calling for "Anarchy in the UK," he managed to amass a political following.

Upon workshopping a draft like this, we could ask Colin's peers to circle places where something feels awkward—missing words, misplaced punctuation, some telegraphed thoughts. But we might as well be honest: Helping Colin perfect the language in this draft will be difficult for most students besides Colin himself. Our real goal should be to get Colin to believe enough in his work to make this next set of changes on his own, out of a commitment to his own writing. At this stage, polishing means trusting that his ideas are there—which they are—and giving himself the time to search for the best words. Students can determine if they are at this stage through a process of elimination—as long as they have outlined clear goals for their essays, based on the demands being placed on them, they, like Colin, will realize at this point that they are at the polishing stage.

EXERCISE 5.3

At the second draft stage, ask students to bring in their papers to small groups. Hand out blue and red pens, and direct groups to exchange and read the essays, underlining strong phrases and sentences with blue ink, and squiggling beneath awkward moments with red ink. The goal here is not to radically reorient the students' project, but make what exists on paper more effective than it already is. After this work has been finished, ask students to take their essays home and modify their sentences for clarity.

If we direct students to keep track of the kind of surface errors frequently marked by their peers and their teachers, they can begin to train themselves over the course of the semester to check for patterns. For example, three or four of the places Colin's classmates marked as awkward were probably instances of comma splices, a grammatical pattern that confuses Colin's sentences throughout his writing. It's important to make a practice throughout the semester, in the classroom and in conferences, of asking students to take a moment to identify the patterns they've noticed in their peer critiques. They can keep track, too, of methods for avoiding the grammatical errors they repeat in a dedicated journal or notebook; in this way, they record a concrete set of strategies to carry out of the classroom with them.

EXERCISES FOR PREPARING STUDENTS TO WRITE BEYOND OUR CLASS

Teaching students to be skilled and confident revisers on their own, and outside the classroom, begins with the training we've illustrated above, but for this training to really gel for students, they must learn to *name* the principles that underlie it. One way to initiate this process is to draw students to articulate those principles that have already helped them the most, and to gather those that seem to have helped the group as a whole. What they can name for themselves, they can use later. The following exercises, which we use toward the end of the semester, lead students to draw on their training to articulate principles that will allow them to become teachers of writing for themselves.

EXERCISE 5.4

Have students jot down the topic of each essay they have written over the course of the semester. What were they trying to figure out in each? What was their main idea? Once they have written a few sentences that synthesize the thinking work of each essay, ask students to describe the writing work—what they were learning about writing during each essay. Then give them a few minutes to look for connections and disjunctions among all their essays, and between the thinking work and the writing work they were doing in each. Discuss.

When reflecting on the exercise above, students are often surprised to discover the obsessions that they have kept secret from themselves—thinking problems that have guided them in various ways throughout the semester, in essays on different topics and in different forms; awareness of their thinking patterns helps them to see more clearly what kind of writers and thinkers they are. And since we teach essay form in a trajectory that begins with familiar essay writing and continues on to more research-oriented academic essays, thinking about how they've worked in each form helps students to identify which writing strategies travel best across their interests, across genres, and across disciplines. Once students have done some writing in response to these prompts, we ask them to discuss together which kind of essay felt more challenging (and why), where the boundaries between the academic and the personal first began to blur for them, and what the mixture of these two forms can offer them in the future.

In the next exercise, we foster an awareness in our students of the way that standards for writing shift from class to class, in order to help them articulate for themselves ways of blending the requirements of any given discipline with the writing techniques they have learned with us.

In Exercise 5.5, we ask students to compare and contrast the writing prompts of their professors. Each student should create a checklist based on this work, including both content-based and formal issues. When the groups have done this, bring students together to discuss what they've discovered. If you've been using checklists in class (such as the one included above), you can frame the discussion by asking where they found themselves writing goals on the checklist similar to goals they've tried to meet in this class, and what their strategies would be to meet those goals. Ask, too, for points of tension between the kind of writing they've done in this class and that which they need to do for the other.

The work with points of tension is crucial to getting students to be good revisers in a range of writing situations. To the extent that they understand the philosophy that undergirds the way they've learned to write in our classes, they can better identify and interpret what their new professors want and how to work with it. There's no pretending that all professors will want the level of complexity, the questioning, or the range of evidence we've been trying to cultivate in our classrooms. As we said in the introduction, our teaching strives not just to make students successful writers, institutionally speaking, but good ones who are generating new thinking in new forms; not all professors want this unless our students can convince them that the

---

EXERCISE 5.5

Have students bring to class a professor's prompt for a paper assignment in another class. Ask them to work in small groups on the following questions: What is each professor asking for? What kind of thinking do they think will be privileged? What kind of thinking might be illegible to that professor? What kind of essay structure does the prompt suggest? What is ambiguous about the paper's requirements? What techniques have they studied in this class that will be helpful in working on this essay?

thinking within such work is effective enough to warrant the new form. Our hope is that we can train students to not only ask the question, "How can I train myself to figure out what professors want?" but to find the wherewithal to write the paper that they want to write. In this respect, it's absolutely crucial that we are in conversation with our students about these issues that inevitably surround the writing they're asked to do in the academy—particularly if they're going to be self-conscious and confident about the choices they make while revising for their classes.

In a final exercise, we provide students with practice in articulating what they value most about their own writing, and how they might draw that work into other settings.

This final exercise can work to break the standard boundary of the class, creating a precedent for experimentation and gradual improvement that continues long after the end of the semester.

These practices help to reveal the form of our class to students, so that they develop their own understanding of their process. Writing is an art that accumulates slowly; it is less characterized by sudden flashes of insight than by incrementally more complex progressions of work, building upon each other with care and time for reflection. In the second part of this book, we will offer three modes of working with progressive models for developing essays in the classroom. Nietzsche (1993) hints at the effectiveness of progressions, as he muses about how writers learn their craft:

> No river is great and abundant of itself; it is the fact that it receives and bears onward so many tributaries that makes it so. . . . All that matters is that one supplies the direction which many flowing tributaries then have to follow, not whether one is poorly or richly gifted from the beginning. (p. 182)

Here we can interpret Nietzsche's writing in two senses: Not only does our teaching aim to supply progressive direction to our students via the shapes of their thought and the forms of their language, but it will succeed by providing the classroom with content designed to make the project of writing abundant. In Part II, we discuss ways of working with progressions that use visual art, culture, and popular culture to make good on this latter goal.

EXERCISE 5.6

Ask students to choose three elements of this writing class that have been most helpful to them—elements that they wish they could transport into any classroom in which they are doing writing. Students may list things like workshopping and conferencing with the teacher, but they should also list methods such as breaking down binary oppositions or examining one's own position, or principles like avoiding treating drafts as finished products. Then ask students to make a plan for how they could create their own personal writing workshop in every class, or on their own. For example, if conferencing with professors is crucial to their most successful essays, they need to challenge themselves to seek out their professors and get the kinds of comments they need.

Part II

CULTURAL FORMS THAT TEACH WRITING

6 *Writing with Visual Art*

We often begin the semester by asking students to engage in a month-long progression that begins with studying a work of visual art and evolves into an essay that incorporates academic readings, stories from personal experience, and aesthetic interpretation of one or more art objects. When we began to send students out to select and study works of art and respond to them in writing, we had only a vague sense that writing about visual texts would jump-start students' imaginations, increase their powers of description, and help them to access more interesting ideas. Over time, we understood that writing with visual art does more than spark creativity: It trains our students to negotiate between their own experience of a cultural object and a multiplicity of possible interpretations. We believe that this kind of negotiation is crucial for good essays in the humanities, and that for this reason, writing with art is a great way to start the semester.

Getting students to enter into this negotiation, however, is tricky business. Often, students' initial written responses to an artwork aren't rich or complicated enough to set a progression toward a good essay in motion. If we send them out without much guidance, students will come back to class having "chosen" the artwork closest to hand—the Monet or Renoir image downloaded from the web, the Robert Doisneau photograph reprinted on the poster in their dorm room—and having written an easy, clichéd description of an image that has already become a cliché in our culture. If they have gone to a gallery or museum and found a good piece of art with which to work, their writing may still be obvious, careful, and stilted. They will have written only what it is possible to write right away. Which brings us back to a familiar problem: When writing on impulse for a college essay, students tend to avoid the exact experience that they most need to have if they are going to generate great writing—not knowing or, in this case, the weighing of multiple possible interpretations.

When it comes to art, this familiar problem is connected to a deeper philosophical issue, for the tendency to pin down the meaning of works of art isn't limited to the classroom. Philosopher Roland Barthes (1977) writes about this issue in his discussion of the captions newspapers place under their photographs, claiming that nowadays the images are the most important thing in news and text is secondary, only there to "quicken" the image, or help us see what it means:

> The [caption's] text constitutes a parasitic message designed to connote the image, to "quicken" it . . . In other words, and this is an important historical reversal, the image no longer illustrates the words; it is now the words which, structurally, are parasitic on the image. The reversal is at a cost . . . in the relationship that now holds, it is not the image which comes to elucidate or "realize" the text, but the latter which comes to sublimate, patheticize or rationalize the image. (p. 25).

It is perhaps this veneration of the image as the most important signifier, in news, advertisements, and other elements of mass media, that trains students to write simple "captions" for the works of art they choose, rather than playing with the multiple meanings that they experience while viewing a piece. And although Barthes isn't talking about artworks, we might extend his thinking here: Artworks *always* say more than any one "explanation" of their meaning can offer, and writers shouldn't seek to "rationalize" images by pinning that meaning down. And yet when we write about art, we are always making claims about what it means, whether we intend to or not.

How can we teach our students to write about art without asking them to describe the artwork once and for all, replicating the problem that Barthes cites in the process? All writing about art is subject to this paradox of interpretation; we believe that it actually provides fertile ground. It is the difficulty provided by this paradox that makes writing with art such a good teaching tool for helping students to be attentive to the texts they read and view, on the one hand, and attentive to themselves and their experience, on the other. The trick is getting students to acknowledge and understand the paradox, and then frame their own writing accordingly.

STRATEGIES FOR HELPING STUDENTS WRITE WITH ART

Our experience has taught us that students are capable of writing in creative and innovative ways with art if they are given the time and the structure in which to experience it on its own terms—and, perhaps more importantly, on *their* own terms. They cannot do this without being given license to experiment, and without being taught that the uncertainty and confusion they feel when challenged by an artwork are assets, rather than limitations.

As teachers, understanding our own experiences of visual art is crucial if we are to assist our students in analyzing the ways in which an artwork creates meanings and negotiates a web of shared and, more often than not, contested cultural values. To fully understand how hard this may be for your students, we invite you to think back to times when you've felt impatient or anxious while viewing artworks, in a museum, say, or a gallery in which you felt everyone was watching you. Do you, like many viewers of art, jump to the knowing comment that sacrifices thinking?

We need to construct a space that ensures that such impatience and anxiety do not devolve into a dynamic where our students latch onto the earliest accessible thesis. Doing so begins with bringing works of art into the classroom and letting students view them up close for prolonged periods of time. It means establishing the classroom as a place where excess is applauded—where the idea of the one "right" interpretation is bracketed for a while, and multiple interpretations can be shared and debated. And it depends on slowing down the process of viewing and interpreting, so that this space renders prolonged thinking and play almost inevitable.

Since our end goal is to get students to select their own piece of art and begin to write outside the classroom, we have to help them cultivate flexible structures for viewing and reflecting that they can take with them out into the world. We conceptualize the process of viewing and writing with art into stages that students should put themselves through as they study a work of art, and we practice these stages all together in the classroom.

A transformation occurs in the time between a student's initial encounter with an artwork and the moment when she develops her interpretation of it. We can imagine this experience as a rite of passage, in three parts:

1. The Initial Encounter, in which the student first observes the artwork in its materiality—studying the piece as it is, without reflecting on it.
2. The Liminal Phase, in which she experiences an excess of possible interpretations and meanings.
3. The End of the Encounter, in which she creatively constructs the multiple interpretations of the work that inspire ideas for an essay.

This passage may occur over the course of the month (while a student writes a paper), or it may take place in a flash of insight, but it is invariably more productive when a student can engage and return to an artwork over time. Our classroom work with single art objects is designed to prolong the different stages of this encounter so that students have time to experience the piece of art on its own terms, entertain many possible ways of thinking about it, and then choose a way to engage with the work. In prolonging this process and celebrating excess, we mean to avoid sacrificing the second stage in a rush to get to the end; we want to keep students from forcibly throwing out all the meanings they encounter that confuse them, or don't fit a simple interpretation. For it is the very excess of meanings produced in the liminal phase that will form the basis of rich and rigorous writing with art.

Phase 1: The Initial Encounter

In class, we ask our students to make a record of the material details of a piece before they are allowed to begin deciding what they think about it. Writers can learn to resist the urge to "find one meaning quick," through naming and reflecting on the details presented by a work of art; this slowing down, this time for merely noticing what is there, establishes a linguistic space for playful interpretations and intellectual argumentation. Without the material details, no space is delineated.

Here are some practices we've developed for guiding the initial encounter, so that students can practice seeing the material artwork as it is:

EXERCISE 6.1

Ask the class to write for 10 minutes, describing as many details as they can observe in the artwork without thinking about the relationships between them or trying to do interpretive work. Then ask them to report these details to the class, and generate a collective list on the board.

- Bring a provocative work of art into the class. (If you cannot gain access to a painting, a poster will work. But if you know artists whose work you like, they will probably jump at the opportunity to have their work viewed and written about by a group of students, especially if you offer to let them read students' responses after the class.)
- Provide ample time to notice the artwork's features. In a classroom, this means giving students several minutes to list as many observable details of the artwork as they can. Urge them to be as creative as possible in what they choose to see. The details they find can range from perspective and color and texture to figures and their poses, positions, and spatial relation to each other.
- Create a space free of surveillance. Write along with your students, doing everything you can to demonstrate that you are not watching over them, but that everyone in the room is grappling with the puzzle of the artwork.
- After everyone has had enough time to write, ask each student to describe a detail of the piece, mentioning some feature that no one else has described. Students will learn to think creatively by listening to the variety of responses.
- Finally, let the aim of class thinking and discussion be geared toward fostering multiplicity—not locating the best all-encompassing description of an artwork, but, rather, celebrating the unending range of elements to be noticed and commented on.

Choosing a provocative artwork is extremely important to making all this happen. In time, students will learn to think and write with almost any kind of piece, but in the early stages of the process, images that include recognizable figures are almost always more accessible and stimulating than their more abstract or conceptual counterparts. A Magritte painting will likely spark a diverse set of interpretations, while a Robert Ryman monochrome may be beautiful in its purity, but will generate a roomful of frowns and not much writing at all. As far as the choosing goes, it's a good idea to pick artworks in terms of how they might work to stimulate writing, rather than on the basis of your personal taste.

Consider the painting by Jules Bastien-Lepage titled *Joan of Arc Listening to the Voices*. In our experience, figurative paintings like this one successfully initiate the process because they offer a range of recognizable objects and relations for students to notice and describe: a young woman standing with an outstretched arm before a low-slung cottage, trees, shrubbery, dirt, a spindle, an overturned stool, and three angels appearing mysteriously in the background. But while the painting has many nameable components, it is so detailed and multilayered that noticing its elements takes some work—you can look at this painting for a long time and continue to see new things.

Phase 2: The Liminal Phase

In his 1969 work *The Ritual Process*, the anthropologist Victor Turner helped spread "liminality" as a concept for explaining the experience of those who participate in rites of passage. For Turner, liminality denotes a period in which participants are "neither here nor there; they are betwixt and between the positions assigned and arrayed by law, custom, convention, and ceremonial" (p. 95). In this sense, the bride and groom in a wedding, those high school students arrayed in

Figure 6.1. *Joan of Arc Listening to the Voices*, Jules Bastien-Lepage. The Metropolitan Museum of Art, gift of Erwin Davis, 1889 (89.21.1).

their graduation gowns, and military cadets can be considered "liminal entities." For the period of the rite of passage, they move "through a cultural realm that has few or none of the attributes of the past or coming state" (p. 94). In their experience with the art that really strikes them, our students will find themselves undergoing a minor "rite of passage"—for the time that they encounter the artwork, they will be on the brink of an interpretation (the "coming state"). And the longer we can keep the encounter active, the better chances we have of making students thinking about artwork effective. The more fruitful the liminal stage, the more productive our students' foundation for writing will be.

When we enact it in the classroom, the goal of the liminal phase is to spend time creating a set of potential provisional connections among the details of the artwork, the evoking tensions that arise therein. Then we ask students to begin speculating playfully about the significance of these connections. We direct students to write a list of questions about what they noticed in the piece only a few minutes earlier, still tethering their writing to the artwork by asking each question in virtue of a detail or relationship in the artwork that anyone could see, if they only looked in the right way.

We offer Exercise 6.2 as a prompt to students before they begin writing. To help students remain between observation and interpretation (or outright value judgments), we instruct the class that any conclusion or declarative sentence is strictly forbidden during this exercise.

After several minutes pass, and students write more and more difficult questions, we push them a bit further by using the prompt in Exercise 6.3. This last reminder ensures that students begin to grapple with the issue of significance without leaving the artwork behind, and serves to direct attention to the students' experience of the artwork as well. In linking the concrete details of the artwork to a series of questions, the class finds itself working in two directions simultaneously. First, in pushing toward questions about the significance of details, the class works toward developing a complicated final interpretation. But at the same time students are looking backward, too, as they interrogate the details of the initial encounter, to the extent that their questions reflect on the features of the artwork they initially observed.

By the end of this very simple exercise, then, our students have begun to do something very complicated: They are noticing details, weighing them against one another, and thereby beginning to reflect on the power and presence of the artwork.

Consider the painting by Lepage that we've used for this exercise. Here are some student questions posed with regard to this painting:

> How many angels, trees, and buildings are there in this painting?
> Why does one of the angels have on armor? Is he holding a sword?
> What is the young woman looking at? Is she holding something?
> Why am I focusing on the woman and not on the trees? Why is it so hard to look at the angels?
> How can there be so much depth in this painting, and yet it be so flat, two-dimensional, in parts?
> Why does it feel so clear that she is listening? Why do I resent the angels so much?

In this way, we ask our students to move from basic details to the problem of significance (and ultimately to their own experiences elicited by the artwork) in a set of questions. If students can begin to interpret the work on the basis of these questions, they will be in a far better place to do the work we will ask of them in the

---

EXERCISE 6.2

In the next 10 to 15 minutes, direct students to ask as many questions as they can of the artwork. No question is too simple. Each question should revolve around a detail in the painting—they may wonder what it is, why it is there, how it relates to other details present in the piece, and so on. Ten minutes is a long time to ask questions about anything, so direct the class to begin with the simplest questions they can imagine, and save the hard questions for the end.

EXERCISE 6.3

Now ask the class to begin asking questions about the most important details they see. Why is one detail more significant than another? Students should write these questions down in terms of how they are interpreting the painting, asking questions like: Why am I concentrating on this detail, rather than that one? Could it have something to do with a hypothesis I already have?

---

final stage—work that aims not to explain what the artwork means, but to generate new ideas arising out of their experience of it. In the final stage, student writing will be related to the artwork, inspired by it, and shed light on its significance without subjecting it to a single, pat interpretation.

Phase 3: The End of the Encounter

In the final exercise, we direct our students to write about the viewing experience itself. But when they do so, we demand that they keep their attention on all the details they've noticed and the questions they've posed, beginning to speculate on what these have to do with their particular experience of the object. Our goal is that they begin to understand and articulate something about the way the artwork effects viewers, but avoid generalizing too simplistically from their own experience by responding to its real presence and power imaginatively.

We ask our students to perform an exercise of focused freewriting, as shown in Exercise 6.4. This final exercise moves our students closer to creating an artwork for themselves, a fiction that explains the power or the presence of the artwork by playfully attempting to recreate the feeling of viewing the work itself.

Here are some excerpts from writings in response to *Joan of Arc Listening to the Voices*:

> Across the sky, just behind the trees, or wait, in front of them, is a series of small fractures. Standing up from my stool, I notice little white lines that cross

---

EXERCISE 6.4

In the next 15 minutes, ask your students to create a fictional scene in which they do not mention the painting. Pick three or four of the details they've noticed, whatever these may be, and use them to create a mood, setting, and story that resonate with your experience of the artwork. Students should write about these details as they would an inside joke, so that anyone in the class will know where they came from, and why, but no one else will. The class should be as creative and imaginative as possible in using experience of the artwork as they strive to leave it behind.

and intersect—like strands from the spindle of wool behind me—stretched over the leaves above me. I have to focus in on them. I cannot tell if they have been there all these years that I have spent in my garden. Have I had a blind spot? Could it have been there all along? My garden is lit anew with an otherworldly glow.

It is not enough to keep spinning this wheel.
It is not enough that the yard is beautiful.
There is something outside that I need.
I am looking nowhere for angels and they are right here.
I have affection for what falls apart.
That is not unreasonable.

I have been haunting this woman for weeks now and she never turns round to notice. I swear I am no stalker, no pervert—I want only to bless her. I'm as innocent as a cherub on a valentine. But I am always watching her, and she is always watching someone else, and it seems to be no person that she is watching—in fact, it is more like she is listening to a voice from another world, that tells her things no one else knows. I want to know what the voice says.

After our students have finished writing this exercise, we all read what we have written. Now that students have attempted to evoke the particular power and presence of this artwork through these fictional scenes, we can help them to begin raising questions about the way meaning gets made in our varied responses to this piece of art. Our goal is to move students toward questions and ideas the significance of which is larger than the individual artwork, but which could not have been communicated without interacting with this particular work. And in this questioning way, we move toward naming the ideas that begin to be born in these scenes— ideas that are not about settling on a final interpretation of the work, nor about returning entirely to one's own experience or previous ideas unchanged, but about something in between the work and the experience.

A crucial last step in this process is moving students from these scenes to the problem generation that will be foundational in their move toward writing an essay. Focusing on one scene a student has written, we have students write down as many different questions as they can that are inspired by the scene. For example, in response to the last scene we might hear questions like these:

Why are we drawn to people we can't understand?
Where do we draw the line between protecting someone and limiting them?
    Why are these two so closely related?
Is watching ever innocent?

We gather as many of these questions as our students can muster on the board, and then ask them to look for connections between the questions, and join two or three of them into a thinking problem the writer might choose to work with. In this case, our students may phrase their problems something like this:

> We watch those we love closely, precisely because we can never totally know them, but cannot stop wanting that total knowledge. This is a paradox of love, and it's unavoidable, but it becomes a problem when our watching limits our love by limiting the one we love. How do we walk this line, and why is the line so narrow?

After coming up with several thinking problems like this one, students have seen the shape of the process we're asking them to initiate with their own chosen work of art. By working in this way, we train students to understand the process of generating an idea as one made easier with free and multilayered play, but one about which they must also be continually making hard decisions. And it is this whole process that we will ask them to repeat in their work with the art they choose to use in their own essays.

As they move from the classroom exercise to writing their own essay, then, we want our students to:

- Understand the new thinking they're doing as the product of a deep engagement of an artwork.
- Honor this engagement in the text of the essay they end up writing by continuing to use description of and conversation with the artwork to develop their ideas.
- Write thick descriptions that attend to the materiality of the piece, so that their readers, like them, can linger with the artwork on its own terms; choose four or five details that they will focus on as they write about the work.

A SAMPLE PROGRESSION FOR WRITING WITH ART

What follows is a progression of exercises that we use across a five-week period to move students incrementally toward writing that uses art to develop a complex idea. After doing this work with students in the classroom, we send students out to repeat it on their own. The first few writing assignments, given over the course of a week or so, will enable them to write with an artwork of their own choosing, using the strategies they've practiced in the classroom. First we suggest a number of

---

PROGRESSION ONE: CONVERSATIONS BEYOND THE GALLERY

CLASS 1—INTRODUCTION TO THE CLASS AND TO PROGRESSION ONE

CLASS 2
Read: Slavoj Zizek, selections from *The Sublime Object of Ideology* (1995), Roland Barthes, *Camera Lucida* (1981)
Write: Write one page comparing and contrasting the aesthetic analyses of Zizek and Barthes. Work to give a thorough account of the essence of their ideas, but organize your writing by your own argument about what's similar and what's different between their

(continued)

PROGRESSION ONE: CONVERSATIONS BEYOND THE GALLERY
(*continued*)

approaches to viewing images. Do not exceed the page limit—study your texts and narrow your argument until you can carry it out in 250 words or less.

CLASS 3

Read: Barthes, selections from *Image/Music/Text* (1977), Sadiya Hartman, selections from *Scenes of Subjection* (1996), John Berger, selections from *Ways of Seeing* (1995).

Research: Begin visiting museums and galleries to find pieces of art that strike you. If you can purchase facsimiles of these works or find them online and print them, it will be helpful over the next weeks.

Journal: Write a description of a piece of art that captures your interest. Without commenting on what you think of the artwork, try to capture as many details as possible at the same time as you evoke the feeling the piece creates. Bring this journal to class so that you can test out your description on your classmates.

CLASS 4

Read: Essays that show writers using images and personal experience to develop ideas: Annie Dillard, "Total Eclipse" (1999), E. B. White, "Once More to the Lake" (2000), Toni Morrison, "The Site of Memory" (2000).

Research: Choose one artwork with which you are fascinated. A good guide for choosing, as we've emphasized in class, is this: Go with the one you're puzzled and intrigued by, not necessarily the one you love.

Write: Following the steps we took in class, respond to the artwork in writing.

1. Write a description of the artwork as it is that anyone would recognize.
2. Then write at least 10 questions about the artwork's meaning; remember to concentrate on the details you see before you as you pose these questions.
3. Keeping as many of these questions as possible in mind, write a fictional scene that expresses your experience of the work; use as many specific details of the piece as you can.

Two to three pages total, typed and double-spaced.

CLASS 5

Read: Essays that develop ideas through a fragmentary style: Richard Rodriguez, "Late Victorians" (2000a), Tim Etchells, "Eight Fragments" (1999), Bernard Cooper, "Burl's" (2000).

Journal: Reflect on the feedback you got in class about your scene; what are the questions and thinking problems that arise from the themes you developed in this description of your experience of the artwork? Write until you've settled on a good first articulation of the preliminary thinking problem you want to explore in this essay.

Write: Choose a method of storytelling from one of the six personal essays that we've read. Then draft a part of your essay in which you write a story from personal experience that develops a new idea in response to the thinking problem you articulated in your journal. You needn't talk about the thinking problem explicitly in this piece; instead, evoke it through the ways in which you choose details carefully, provoke sensory experience, and imitate the narrative techniques your essayist employs. At least three pages, typed and double-spaced, please.

CLASS 6

Journal: Write a list of questions you have about your thinking problem. These questions should be framed to invite thinking and reflection, not research. Then choose an essay, from among the 11 we've read together, that helps you to address some of these questions.

Write: Craft a part of your essay in which you do three things (not necessarily in this order—the more you can move back and forth among these three requirements, the more you'll push your thinking along):

1. Give a sustained description of your artwork that articulates your latest, best version of your thinking problem, while recreating at the same time the drama of the image;
2. Develop that thinking problem through several pieces of evidence, to show its importance (stories from personal experience, other art objects, pieces of pop culture—anything that feels connected and helps you to think about the significance of this problem to people other than you); each new piece of evidence should help you to develop a new idea about the problem, but work, too, to connect these ideas together, building each one on the one before;
3. Choose one of the thinkers we have read and summarize their essay, borrowing and building on the thinker's ideas to develop a provisional theory about your thinking problem.

CLASS 7

Read: Model student essay "Fathers and Sons."
Write: Review the idea that you developed through the story you wrote for Class 5. In your journal, write questions and doubts you have about that idea. Draft a part of your essay in which you do these three things, though not necessarily in this order:

1. Write another story, in tension with the last one—a memory from personal experience that enables you to doubt and question your initial idea.
2. Introduce, summarize, and connect this to a new (i.e., you didn't write about it in your last exercise) idea from the professional essay you've chosen to work with.
3. Return to the work of art, developing a new connection between it and your stories, with the help of the new thinking you've drawn out of your professional essay.

CLASS 8

Write: First rough draft due
Suggested steps for writing a rough draft:

1. Read your last three exercises on the computer, cutting sentences and paragraphs that no longer seem smart or necessary to you. Cut and paste the remaining parts into one document.
2. Print that document. Cut it up with scissors into as many parts as makes sense, then play with these parts on your desk or on the floor until you start to see a progression of ideas, albeit with some parts missing.

(continued)

PROGRESSION ONE: CONVERSATIONS BEYOND THE GALLERY
(*continued*)

3. Keep notes on what's missing—new parts you need to write, claims you need evidence for, questions that go long unanswered, connections between paragraphs, thinking moves that need to be made more explicit, ideas that need to be developed, and sections that need to be written. Could you use more personal perspective? More work with your written text?
4. Draw a chart, drawing, or diagram of your essay, illustrating how one idea leads to the next.
5. Write the missing parts.

Remember: Bring two copies of your rough draft to class, unless you've volunteered to have your draft read by everyone, in which case you should bring 16 copies.

CLASS 9
Read: Five of your classmates' essay drafts; using the checklist we developed in the last class as a guide, comment thoroughly in the margins and throughout the text of each, write a one-paragraph end comment recommending revision strategies, and provide your name and e-mail in case the writer needs to contact you for explanation. Come to class ready to discuss all five essays in detail.

CLASS 10
Final draft due.

---

galleries and museums and ask them to choose one, visit it, and select a piece of art that intrigues, excites, and/or puzzles them. Their writing assignments will take them, again, through the stages of the rite of passage they've performed in the classroom: describing the material object with elaborate and detailed attention to all its elements, raising questions linked to these elements and wondering about the relationships between them, and fictionalizing the particular power and presence of the piece. We then help them mine this writing for larger ideas and questions they want to explore, with the help of some other written texts and their memories of personal experiences that seem connected to the artwork. When they draft their final essays, we challenge them to write about the piece of art with which they began this whole process in a way that respects the challenge the artwork presents in and of itself, but allows the writer creative and intellectual authority in interrogating the experience of viewing that piece for his or her readers.

Our goal in this progression has been to stave off the moment of decision—when the writer chooses the ideas the painting inspires—until our students have written something that is at once both their own and the product of a conversation with an artwork's concrete features. If this set of exercises works well enough in the classroom, our students will have initiated a deep and rewarding inquiry into how the artwork came to effect their imaginations. With these methods and experiences behind them, downloading the first image that surfaces on the Internet and tossing off a description may seem less valuable than finding a meaningful work of art to experience for themselves. They will be a step closer to more engaged, pleasurable, and challenging experiences in galleries and museums, on the one hand, and more rigorous and imaginative writing, on the other.

What follows is an exemplary essay from this progression. We'll ask you to notice in particular the way Ted Mann has worked with an artwork, which inspired the thinking problem of his essay, to develop ideas about that problem and to provide the language that binds the entire essay together. He introduces the artwork—a painting by Winslow Homer of a fisherman at sea—midway through, after establishing his theme and some of his questions through stories from personal experience. In his introduction of the artwork we can see evidence that he has lingered long enough in the initial encounter to be able to evoke the material painting in a detailed, vivid way. But he has also edited his initial description of the work, using carefully chosen adjectives and verbs to foreshadow the ideas he will later develop.

While in his first paragraph of description Ted has stayed very close to the original artwork, depicting it in a way that most any viewer would agree with, in his next paragraph he begins to raise questions inspired by the painting. His questions are mostly psychological—he wants to know what's going on in the fisherman's head, and because the artwork does not provide him with easy answers, he begins to imagine possibilities. In this paragraph we can see the remnants of the liminal stage, in which the student is entertaining multiple interpretations.

As Ted continues, he's inspired by a familiarity, a connection between the painting and his life. And so the questions raised by looking at Homer's painting begin to seep out into his memories, and he reproduces this movement for his readers as he leaves the painting behind. The foundation for this movement is the work in the final stage that he has done in class and on his own, in which he practiced dramatizing the particular presence and power of the piece.

Ted focuses in on one aspect of the painting, the fisherman's beard, to evoke the feeling he gets from the artwork, and to begin to connect it to personal experience. His essay continues on to investigate problems surrounding middle-aged masculinity, and the painting provides a touchstone for this investigation. He weaves the language of his initial description throughout his essay, using boating, fishing, and being caught in a storm as metaphors for the struggles of his father, and of everyone's fathers. In doing so, he is not pinning down the meaning of the painting, but instead questioning his experience of the painting and what it tells him about fatherhood and middle age.

STUDENT ESSAY

Fathers and Sons
by Ted Mann

My father knows the beach, not boats. He did not have that kind of childhood, the one drenched in frigid water and frosted in salt, smelling of mussels and pine and varnish, that I wanted so badly for myself. He was born in Yonkers but raised in Los Angeles; he knows the surf and the far-off turquoise of the Pacific. I have a Pacific father, and I am his Atlantic son.

A friend once remarked of his father's life, "There's really nothing more sad than that middle-aged, divorced, bachelor pad." I knew what he was saying and my dad would, too. The pathetic sight of a middle-aged father cut adrift is almost too much for either of us to take.

My mother and father finally agreed to divorce each other when I was in the fourth grade. The bizarre process of moving out consisted of several mutual friends coming over to help pack the necessities into a car and to crack a few jokes about unrelated topics before driving away with someone who had been my father. No one seemed to have any appropriate words for the children, so there was a lot of bashful head-tousling and patting everyone's shoulders. Even at that age, not yet frosted by cynicism, I found the entire process ridiculous.

The first apartment was a sad affair, the first floor of a firetrap rooming house adjacent to the biggest shopping center in Ardmore, where we gathered on either Tuesdays or Thursdays and every other weekend to eat pasta off plastic plates and sometimes watch *The Cosby Show* if our homework was finished. My father, a man once terrifying in anger, was a converted caver-in, relaxing rules and acting sheepish in the hopes that we would not be loath to return. At the same time, we the children had our own role, a turncoat tattletale act that meant making wherever we were not seem like the very gates of Hades, with flames, no smoke detectors, and fleas, most likely, too. The impulse of a divorced parent to try to ease his child's mind is matched only by that of his children to make him feel competent, like his better half. And we did love my dad's "house." After all, we never had to do the dishes, we got to see Bill Cosby on Thursdays, and we had the blue Crest toothpaste that sparkled. This divorce thing was not so bad sometimes.

My father sailed off course. A man with few vices, he did not have any of the more interesting depression pastimes to turn to, like drinking scotch in a darkened room with the shades down, or getting into fist fights at work. Instead he seemed caught up in the observation of his condition, as if what was happening was so strange and frightening that he could only stare at it as it swept him off the course that had once seemed to be unchanging. He gave in more. I broke one of the windows in the garage door trying to throw a curve with a tennis ball, then claimed to have hit the bottom of the wood, just above the ground. "I think it just sort of rattled out," I said. He looked at me with the old look, as if he were standing on a ladder, waiting for another lie to slip out, when he would descend upon me like nobody's business and make me start to love telling the truth. His eyebrows, raised in a gesture of menace and expectation, suddenly fell. Anger evaporated, leaving behind the residual expression of defeat. "It's an old door," said my father. "Whyn't you guys throw against the other side of the garage?"

In one of Winslow Homer's more famous paintings, a fisherman alone in a dinghy is caught by a fast moving storm, a cloud of fog crushing in from the horizon. The sun is being smothered, the whitecaps on the swells leaping eagerly, and the wave beneath his boat rocks it aside, about to slam it down into the next trough. The fisherman is not frantic, though. His oars are poised above the water, held steadily outward by strong, thick wrists. The man, in his drenched brown canvas jacket and pants, studies the clouds. His beard, his shoulder, his eye, all point toward the horizon, toward the mucous-yellow light swallowed by a fog of purplish-gray. The fog steams off the water at the horizon, as if the sea is boiling out there and will soon scald the staring man in his errant boat. Out behind him, the larger fishing boat, from which he has launched his dinghy, streams away under full sail, threatening to disappear and leave him to fight the coming storm on his own with only his instincts and a pair of oars.

The wave that snatches the dinghy also pulls it away from the larger boat, in the opposite direction, and yet the man does not seem to take full notice: he is unaware of the instantaneous danger of the clouds. Does he even care about the menace of the storm? Face upturned into the bruising clouds, does he care about his death, or just the unexpected beauty of a natural, irresistible force? The fisherman watches the storm come to get him, waits for a moment, taking stock of his enemy. He forms a clear image in his mind of the storm which will sink him to the ocean floor; he has paused a second too long. His chances of escape have dwindled to nothing as he stares stoically at the approaching clouds.

It is my father's beard. The man in the boat has my father's beard; he strikes the pose of my father at his Sunday morning baseball games, watching a fly ball to right field from third base, neck turned almost ninety degrees, body still facing forward, ready to snatch a ground ball. There are other similarities. My father was cut adrift from his life, and it was just as much his fault as this fisherman's, who seems to have strayed too far in search of bigger fish. And now the two of them pause when they should act, take a deep breath when they should sprint or row. They should sustain the pace of that boat out there, that past enthusiasm for and dedication to being alive. But they are not, or have not yet started, and I cringe at the sight like the blonde cheerleader opening the closet door in any high school horror film. Now it is too late.

It was not too late. I should have known as much from knowing his father, he of nine times over Bremen, leaky valves in the heart, and now a wife who has forgotten his face. My father rented a house on Lowry's Lane, number 123, a tiny building with built-in ants and three bedrooms, and someone else's trash and mementos in the basement. He was only a bike ride away now. He was almost back.

Most children talking about divorce, at least those documented by the authorities who write the self-help books, speak endlessly about the prayers they have said to reunite mother and father. Then comes the blurb by a licensed psychiatrist or therapist or faith healer explaining that Mommy and Daddy don't love each other any more. You are still a family, they tell me, but now a family with two houses. Thank you for explaining, I think. I had not noticed. The wish for a beautiful compromise between the two warring parties is one that I never thought I had. I had expected my parents to divorce since the first time I ever heard them argue, really argue, during an ugly drive across Arizona many years ago. I did not expect them to fall back in love, to return to each other on, say, Christmas Eve, to burst into Christmas carols and make merry around the tree until we all expired from pure happiness. I also did not expect either one of them to get married.

The man off-course found a commiserator and mate in a woman who had once taught gardening and elementary school and was thinking of becoming a paralegal. She had three children. She had been married twice. To them, it was the serendipitous encounter of unique and beautiful people. To me, it was revolting and a terrible idea.

To think of my father's remarriage as a necessary stage in the continuing life of the middle-aged, jettisoned man helps a little. Remarriage is an inaccurate term, however: my father has not re-married my mother; he is married, but it is to another place and space, to another family as well as to another woman. He has his family, and I am still a part of it, but now I have company. His family, as he pictures the word, now contains nine people. Mine is just a rotating lineup of five, with either my mother or father batting cleanup. Far from the *Brady Bunch*, although equal in size, my two-nights a-week family is a conglomerate of two very different corporations, who constantly cite the old way of doing business as next to heaven and fight each other for the remote control. There has never been hate among us but the house has swelled to bursting at times with pride and insecurity, the children not relinquishing faith in the lives they had previously known. I care for my step-family; I accept them and defend them, but I can never know the bedtime stories of their infancy. They can never know mine.

Accepting a step-family is not the hard part. The difficulty is that they don't know the inside jokes, the rules for who gets to ride in the front seat, the names of the dogs. They don't understand or revere the trivialities of the family that has just been pulverized. To my father, the radical differences of "my" family and his must have been soothing. The new household was set in its ways, but still must have seemed like a clean slate, a second chance at nuclear family. The fisherman, once frantic and lost, had found a way out of the storm. He was rowing in a new way, trolling for different fish and still trying to keep pace with the disappearing ship on the horizon, but at least he was starting once again.

At the end of the summer before I went to college, my father and I packed two bags apiece and drove to Cleveland. We spent a week on the road, driving and avoiding tractor-trailers, in the heady pursuit captured by *Field of Dreams*. In that movie, a grown man, whose relationship with his amateur baseball player father disintegrated during adolescence, builds a baseball field to attract the ghost of Shoeless Joe Jackson. The field he thinks he is building for Shoeless Joe turns out to be for none other than the ghost of his father, in uniform and catcher's gear. The real fruit of the whole enterprise is the game of catch the man finally plays with his father. It is a pageant staged for fathers and sons according to Hemingway's depiction of that relationship: here is an easy, restrained way for two strong-willed men to express love, and undeniably weak emotion. The love lost between a growing man and his aging role model is regained in the pop of leather and the smell of tradition. Few words are exchanged; the scene's power lies in the simple action of throwing and receiving. Despite the stormy arguments that frequent adolescent–parent interaction, my relationship with my father has never been washed away. Our time together was already limited by mortality and custody agreements; there was not enough to waste storming out of the house and vowing not to return. Our trip was not intended to be remedial. We were looking for baseball and thought our motives were that simple. But baseball is essentially a confounding game, always managing to mean more to you than you suspect or hope it does.

As other traditional hallmarks of masculine youth have fallen out of favor, replaced by convenience, by novelty, baseball has clung against all odds to the shirttails of American adult men. It is the game their fathers gave them. It reminds them of the first time they won anything, of the day their fathers had to quit pitching underhand to them. They remember when they first realized that they were better than their fathers at the game they inherited. What we chased through the Midwest was more than "quality time"; we knew, as a salmon knows the way home, that there was something awaiting us at the end of the highway, a peace with no war to precede it. Somewhere in Illinois, or in Ohio, rain rattling the window trim, we would arrive at a peace between us, forgiveness of the son for stealing youth.

So we drove. We saw the Indians play the Orioles, the Tigers against the Athletics, the Cubs beat the Cardinals, and the Pirates struggle with the Dodgers. We drove and slept and searched for cheap motels. We shared stadium peanuts, got fat from hot dogs and the occasional beer. We screamed in stadiums four times my age the cheers of my father at eighteen— and didn't have to say much beyond that. The notion that this was the last vacation, the end of being a son and of being a protective father, was left unsaid, but it was said in the recounting of baseball games and my father's offhand stories from college. It was easier just to feel, to say without stating, the unrest of inevitable change.

After our final game, I dropped him off at the airport for a business flight and prepared to drive his car home. I could not avoid feeling that he had left something in the trunk, that I was somehow taking an important piece of luggage from him that would be gone forever, that he needed not just to live but to exist in time and memory. I turned around in my seat at the first red light and looked into the back of my father's car. A map book, a red club, a cooler full of melted ice and spilled Sprint. Six days' worth of newspapers consumed entirely. Nothing of his was missing; all his bags were with him. I turned back to face the road. The sun was appearing from behind fog in the Allegheny Mountains. I rolled down the window and aligned my left arm along the top of the door like my father. I drove to Philadelphia. In the rearview mirror, the woolen fog frayed in the light, like a thousand times before.

The disruption of the family that comes shuffling hand-in-hand with divorce sometimes breaks the communication of parents and children. Some children peer out the back of the boat to find that their father's rowboat has disappeared. Some fathers survive the sudden storm and find themselves alone. The father wonders how he will ever pass on his knowledge and the traditions of his family to his sons. He realizes that he will never have the moment with which he associated fatherhood: waking up next to his son's mother, announcing that he and his child will be gone for a few days, off in the woods or at the ballpark, the boy imitating a man, the father reliving boyhood. How will the divorced, bi-weekly father hold his son's attention long enough to have the man-to-man talks he has been preparing his whole life to give? The nuclear family is supposed to be the only way to ensure that imparting of wisdom and experience to one's children.

Americans cherish the rite of "man-to-man." But does the father really teach his son as much as we assume? How could so many good fathers have produced so many confused ones? Consider the target audience for *Field of Dreams*, which tweaked a nerve in the moviegoer's spinal column and became a blockbuster. A man's monument to his heroes is necessitated by the dearth of communication that plagues his relationship with his father. The audience embraced it because they recognized that theme and could affirm its existence in their own lives; middle-aged men saw the reconciliation of late father and adult son as the opportunity many wished they had had. Not to talk, but to not have to talk, to return to a time in life when the simple gestures of a backyard catch calmed the ugliest tantrums and erased the angry words they wished to take back. That audience had once simply solved problems by hanging out with Dad, by throwing a baseball, or going to a ballgame. Where had the easy answers gone?

The relationship between son and father is never easily navigable. The inevitability of the son's eclipsing his predecessor hangs like fog over their relationship, thickening into a storm as the child becomes a man. E. B. White (1971) writes of these emotions in his essay, "Once More to the Lake." The middle-aged writer, on returning to the scene of his boyhood summers with his son, is amazed not at the changes the lake has undergone, but at its enduring similarities. He listens to his son sneaking out in the early morning to explore by canoe just as he had. He watches as his child is caught up in the net of summer, drinking soda, watching girls, and collapsing into bed, exhausted, not long past sunset. All of these activities the elder White remembers from his days as an adolescent. He recalls the feeling of exploring and being old enough to explore on his own.

White remembers his father's role in the vacations of childhood and is startled to find himself acting out the part. The father grows confused in his role; was he not still a son? "I began to sustain the illusion that he was I," White writes, "and therefore, by simple transposition, that I was my father" (p. 723). The boy has stolen White's place in his own memory. His son has run off with something of his father's still in the backseat; a transposition is taking place in increments. What started with the birth of the son will end with the death of the father; the father strives to raise a son only to be replaced by him. White's essay is not a meditation on his lake of choice so much as the revelation of a truth which all fathers bear: they have procreated; they have done their duty; the next adventure will lead into death. Hemingway said that achieving fatherhood was the death of a man, and similarly, White realizes that through the conception of his replacement, he has given away his boyhood, and now must follow his own father into death: "As he buckled the swollen belt suddenly my groin felt the chill of death" (p. 727).

E. B. White found himself staring into an abyss of feeling, feeling not the waves of memory, of being someone's son, but the relative vacuum of being someone's father. The task of raising children, done, leaves death as the only unexplored frontier. The boy who grew before him was his actual life's work, his reason for existing. Like my father, his son had started to steal his father's memories. My father leaning on a wall in a hotel room, watching me pack a suitcase for the day's driving, no longer sees himself doing the same thing thirty years before. I have fogged up his memory with my presence; when the fog lifts, that past will be mine.

The flailing man, feeling dismissed from family, removed from fatherhood and a position of influence over his children, believes he feels more acutely the confusion and pain of giving over to adulthood the only children he'll ever have. My father would say that no intact family could know his bruised emotions. The jettisoned father, however, mourns the same loss of memory as does E. B. White, as all fathers must.

As children of "fractured" families, we are taught that we are stronger for having experienced unusual hardship in personal life, for having grown up in circumstances that will make us permanently skeptical of love and marriage, even of parenthood, if we are not careful to enunciate every day the sanctity of love and the anomaly of our parents' discord. But adolescence spares no illusion, leaves no principle unquestioned in any family. The relationship of parents, married or otherwise, is never safe from the scrutiny and doubt of the child who is being asked to emulate their attempt at family. For the parents as well, the sudden appearance of themselves in their children reflects on their own characters and motives. Bringing up an adolescent must invariably call into question the life of the guardian.

My father, after a long period of imbalance and unsure footing, found gravity in a new household, with a new wife and a new way of thinking about family. He did not succumb to the tempest that threatened to swallow him, but rather sailed out on a new tack, having found another path to take him in the same direction. Any father must undergo the trauma of bidding his children to overtake him, must watch in wonder as his son, despite countless warnings, repeats the mistakes of the father and lives the same adventures. Living two miles from my father for almost nine years has not estranged us. The tension of replacement that plagues all fathers and sons infects the two of us as well. We are not mutated by the stigma of divorce. In the end, I will overtake him, as he has surpassed my grandfather by assuming the role of the parent. Eventually, it is I who will stand at an airport somewhere, suitcase in hand, feeling a bizarre jealousy and terrible anxiety as my son pulls away in the family car, left arm trailing out the window, eyes on the rearview. I have not stolen something from my father; he has given something precious away.

The first time I came home from college, for a weekend, I went to my father's house and found him on the couch. He groaned slightly as he stood up to greet me. He told me he had been playing baseball earlier and thought he might have pulled a muscle or something. "Went four for six, though." We both smiled, and he flicked the bill of my cap, knocking it backwards over my head and onto the floor. "Hey," he called out as we began to grapple, "I'm not as old as you think."

WORK CITED

White, E. B. (2000). Once more to the lake. *Encounters: Readings and the World* (P. C. Hoy II and R. DiYanni, Eds.). New York: McGraw-Hill.

7 *Writing Between Cultures*

I came to theory desperate, wanting to comprehend—to grasp what was happening around and within me.

—bell hooks, *Teaching to Transgress*

When students enter college, they are asked to study texts, histories, perspectives, positions, and ideas different from their own. They're required by their classroom discussions and papers to interact with cultural difference in thoughtful ways. For many students, however, the sheer difficulty of thinking outside of their own position in the world leads them to respond to difference in reactionary or reductive ways. Rather than dismissing these responses as unrelated to more mature or ethical thinking, it's important to understand students' initial reactions to cultural difference as default modes that, once recognized, can teach them to approach the issues in more complicated, rigorous, and dialectical ways. Particularly positioned to help students perform this work of self-reflection, the writing classroom can also benefit from the way that the philosophical issues that surround cultural difference provide complex problems that, when articulated well, help to inspire intellectually nuanced thinking.

In this second progression, we prepare students to do this work in the university by asking them to engage with culture in ways that move them out of their zone of comfort—that handful of positions and views that they too often take as unassailable facts about the way they live. We invite them to write about a heated political issue, and encourage them to think about that issue through the lens of personal experience and with the help of theorists, employing thinking moves that expose gaps and possibilities in the ways they have previously thought. Once we have shaken these preferred methods of thinking and beliefs about the world, we can help our classes discover that writing about culture is every bit as "creative" as writing with art. But before we discuss how we make this happen, we should mention some essential aspects of how we handle the issue of cultural difference in the classroom.

What do we mean by "culture," and by "difference"? When we ask them to examine their culture, first-year college students may wonder, for good reason, what kind of analysis we want to see performed. Students often assume that "culture" refers to what other groups have—that culture only belongs to those who are "different." For example, students whose ethnicity is unmarked in the United States—i.e., students who are white—may ignore their imbrication in cultural dynamics, especially if they assume "culture" means "race" (and for many, "race" excludes "white"). For these students, the beliefs, mores, and implicit judgments of their own culture may seem utterly invisible, causing them to claim that though some people are defined by cultural characteristics, they themselves are not. For others, their own difference so defines their relation to culture that their race, gender, or class may seem altogether too visible, so that they long to ignore, rather than examine, their position in the world.

READING THE STRUCTURES OF DEFAULT THINKING PATTERNS

How can we avoid the habits of reduction that encourage students to leave their own positions in the world unexamined? The best solution may be through dialectics. Sometimes the best way to get students to examine their own culture, and how they act within it, is to draw them to think about cultures other than their own. But to draw students to write smart essays on cultural topics, the opposite is also true: Student claims about other cultures will remain facile if their own cultural positions remain unexamined.

Examining the default modes through which students tend to interact with perceived cultural difference can provide us with some strategies for involving students in productive dialectical approaches. Consider a typical example: In a student–teacher conference about his essay on cultural stereotypes, a student of ours explained his belief that his stereotypes about people from other races and cultures are often "correct." His evidence was a recent experience in a "diversity workshop" sponsored by the university during freshman orientation. During the workshop, the student, who is white, was paired with a female African-American student, and they were asked to write a list of their assumptions about each other. According to the student, he and his partner were happy to report that they had precisely described the other's tastes, interests, and beliefs, simply by generalizing from what they could see about each other. For this student, the workshop that had been designed to create surprise—to make him question his ready assumptions about people who are different from him—only served to cement his notion that he could always trust his assumptions about race, class, and gender: that he could unproblematically know people, no matter their difference from him.

If we reflect on the structure of our student's thinking, we see a contradictory double movement. On the one hand, he is applying generalized assumptions to a unique case, as is his partner, when they define each other only through each other's similarities to cultural stereotypes. On the other hand, he is taking this experience of (superficially) successful identification and applying it to all circumstances in which there is cultural difference. He is committing what rhetoricians call a *metonymic fallacy* and doing it in two directions at once: letting a whole stand for a part, and a part stand in for a whole.

This structure of generalizing from one's experience, of course, is one in which prejudice and close-mindedness can thrive. But within the shell of this form is a kernel of truth, for it is only in finding isolated events exemplary of larger dynamics, and in using larger dynamics as a lens through which to see isolated events, that we can write about culture at all. It is not the structure of generalization itself, but the way in which writers carry their thinking out that is limited or productive. Unless we're clear about this distinction with our students, they will likely be confused (or even angry) when, for example, we ask them to stop generalizing from particular situations—and then turn around and ask students to generalize, but in the "right" way.

WRITING THROUGH METONYMY

In the last chapter, we concentrated on working with an art object in isolation, and suggested that the techniques employed in analyzing art would carry over into the various kinds of work asked of our students as their college careers unfolded. The practice of lingering on the complexities of a single object does much to prepare students to write about culture; for just as we demanded that they pay attention to a singular art object in order to mine their experience for tensions that could lead to ideas, so here we want students to remain attentive to the particularities of cultural objects and events long enough to become involved in a complex thinking problem. Now we want to ask students to build upon this thinking and take their writing a step further, by analyzing the cultural dynamics in which a particular object or event participates.

Steven Greenblatt's (1996) definition of culture is helpful in this regard; he suggests that students think of "culture" as a shared dynamic of "movement and constraint" in our lives, a paradoxical situation in which we are both held back and freed by our relation to a governing body, whether that is a tradition, a family, a government, or, even more to the point, to a body that we do not even perceive as governing our actions (but is involved in how we behave nonetheless). By his description, the average person is governed less often by the "spectacular punishments reserved for serious offenders . . . [than by] seemingly innocuous responses: a condescending smile, laughter poised between the genial and the sarcastic . . ." (pp. 225–226). For Greenblatt, subtle instances of positive and negative reinforcement act as the primary form of culture at any particular level, whether that's the culture of consumerism, of Aborigines in Australia, of opera, of the academy. Thus it is not explicit rules, laws, or "police" that demonstrate the most important aspects of how our cultures work. Instead, it is in soft social policing, such as that done by a "condescending smile," that a culture passes on its values.

One strategy for helping students to think through the dynamic of culture is to have them begin with those subtle moments in which this soft social policing happens. In choosing these moments, we are asking them to write through *metonymy*. A metonymy is a condensation of meanings onto one local moment, object, or word. We might think about it as a process like that of making a reduction in cooking. When you boil a concoction down so that the water is evaporated and what is left is the condensed essence of the thing, a supersaturated solution results. The whole is there, but it's intensified in this smaller part. At the same time, the part does not claim to "stand in for" the whole—as our examples show later in this chapter, when used effectively, professional writers use metonymy to be suggestive without committing themselves to false generalizations. In our classes, we use the term rather loosely: This kind of thinking could be invested in locating synecdoche (where the part really does stand in for the whole), or creating metaphors. Our hope is that our students will discover how condensed symbols can help them to write through general problems in a more specific and effective manner. This work will lead us into the productive paradox of metonymy, which is also the crucial paradox for student work with cultural evidence: The deeper students can travel into the details of, and the differences within, a particular piece of evidence, the more they can say about universal problems and dynamics without simplifying them or making too-general claims.

How can we teach students to write through metonymy without treating their metonymic evidence as simplistically representative of larger dynamics? Contemporary theorists, most prominently Jacques Derrida, have pointed to the ways in which metonymical relationships can create meaning that is not pinned down. Given attentive work with the details of a metonymic moment or text, students can speak to universal problems and dynamics without making claims about what is always the case, everywhere; the thinking we want them to do is about locating the similarities and differences between the metonymic moment and other moments in which similarly condensed meanings are found.

Artists and writers are masters of metonymic thinking; they tell stories or paint pictures of the world that are clearly representative of wider issues—microcosms, if you will, of problems and experiences too vast to consider in a few pages or a single canvas. Consider, for instance, how Jamaica Kincaid (2000) uses a description of her father's hat in the essay "On Seeing England for the First Time." In this essay, Kincaid is interested in describing the vast dominance of British culture over her native Antigua. She writes:

> My father, who might have sat next to me at breakfast, was a carpenter and a cabinet maker. The shoes he wore to work would have been made in England, as were his khaki shirt and trousers, his underpants and undershirt, his socks and brown felt hat. Felt was not the proper material from which a hat that was expected to provide shade from the hot sun should be made, but my father must have seen and admired a picture of an Englishman wearing such a hat in England, and this picture that he saw must have been so compelling that it caused him to wear the wrong hat for a hot climate most of his long life. And this hat—a brown felt hat—became so central to his character that it was the first thing he put on in the morning as he stepped out of bed and the last thing he took off before he stepped back into bed at night. (p. 352)

Here, Kincaid's hat stands as a metonym for a larger social construction—England's undeniably stifling cultural influence over her native Antigua, and her father's desire for the values that it presented. By using the hat in much the same way that students used their experience of the artwork in Chapter 6, not taking it for a given, but questioning the way it suggests values and conflicts, Kincaid is able to avoid easy claims about society. Instead, she provides us with a greater understanding of a complex and contradictory dynamic at work in her own native Antigua—namely, the desire of her community, and she herself, to enjoy the very form of British cultural domination that effectively prevents them from celebrating Antiguan history and values.

In order to make metonymy work when writing about culture, our students need to learn how to do two essential things:

1. Choose well. To do this, they must be able to distinguish significant and multilayered cultural events from events that are one-sided or otherwise too simple to invoke a meaningful link to a social dynamic.
2. Interpret slowly. They must be able to resist settling on their simplistic initial interpretations, which reduce connections among pieces of evidence to their lowest common denominator.

In the next sections of this chapter, we will concentrate on improving the quality of our students' thought as they begin to make connections between their interpretations of cultural objects and events and the dynamics they have teased out of such singular examples.

STRATEGIES FOR WORKING WITH METONYMY IN THE CLASSROOM

In class, we perform the exercises and questions provided below to help students initiate not only a search for compelling cultural metonymies, but also early connections that could foster compelling applications to wider dynamics.

- Ask students to freewrite about a time in which they felt constrained by family or friends against doing something that they wanted to do. In writing such an assignment, ask students to fill in as much of the context as possible, imagining not only what it felt like to be constrained, but also what motivations family and friends might have had in governing their behavior.
- As students read their pieces aloud, ask the class to write down whether or not the story resonates with their own experience, and what other situations they might compare this one to.
- During the discussion period, ask the class to mark their favorite or most complicated moments in each student's story, and then explain why that "key moment" might be symbolically important in excess of the author's intention. Our aim here is to become playful with the various key moments our students pick, in order to help the writer discover new possibilities for analyzing their anecdotes. In this sense, we are hoping for too many suggestions from the class, an abundance of possibilities for the student writer's consideration.
- Brainstorm about possible dynamics that other specific (though ostensibly unrelated) situations might share with the piece.
- Discuss why certain moments in given stories need to be examined or teased out more fully in order to make a metonymy possible.

When we have practiced this work together in the classroom with personal experiences the students have had, we send them out to search for more cultural artifacts and moments in their own lives that can function as metonyms for important dynamics in their culture. These important moments will allow for charged, detail-driven writing that will offer broad argumentative power for the essays that our class will develop late.

FINDING THE BLIND SPOT

To push students into the next stage of the questioning process, we ask them to find the "blind spot" in their interpretations of a metonymic moment or event. For if we can spur our classes to look for that unseen other side of the story, we can motivate them toward more rigorous and truthful interpretations of their examples. It is in this work with blind spots that complex new understandings of cultural dynamics often unfold for students, for the shock of discovering what aspects of the story they have sacrificed, without knowing it, invariably leads them to further thinking. To make this happen, we encourage our students to find an opposing interpretive angle that has slipped beneath their radar screens. Such inverted positions are easy to drum up, and they can be exceptionally useful if the teacher can cultivate a spirit of play (rather than merely a "devil's advocate" opposition). The spirit of play is easier to achieve early in an essay's development, but after homework assignments have been written about the cultural moments or objects that the class has begun to mine for questions and ideas. In other words, students must have done enough writing to have begun to interpret the meaning of their metonymy, but if they are too far along, they may be resistant to modifying their thinking.

Examples of working with blind spots are listed below:

- In considering the way masculinity functions in a John Wayne movie, we might ask students to think of the way femininity functions, too. By focusing on the less obvious role in the western, students may find a more condensed symbol for the ways that gender is constructed in such films.
- If a students write about the symbolic implications of a quite common act (say, cheating on a test), we might ask them to consider what they think was *uncommon* about the behavior. In the cheating case, we may ask whether the example is indicative of a perceived necessity (the common interpretation)—a sense that the student *needed* to cheat in order to succeed—or if cheating occurs "for the thrill of it," out of the desire to sneak around a system of arbitrary checkpoints and hoops to jump through (the uncommon interpretation). By drawing students to look for idiosyncratic, surprising implications, we can help them envision radically different kinds of arguments, new ways of looking at common events.

Once a metonym has been marked, we ask our students to shift and modify their thinking to take full advantage of the dynamic and its implications. Essays that interrogate dynamics move away from only aiming to "solve" a simple problem. They teach our students habits for making an effort to unearth diverse causes for the problems they are encountering, and marking what is at stake in the dynamics they have uncovered. Once this work is undertaken, students are positioned to develop arguments without risking oversimplification.

MARKING THE TRIAD BETWEEN RACE, CLASS, AND GENDER

A third stage in "opening up" our students' interpretive approaches to their cultural artifacts occurs when we ask students not only to mark new ways of thinking about the object or event itself, but also to render visible and problematize their most basic interpretive frame for thinking through cultural issues. For essays that investigate culture, the most common triad used in the liberal arts is that of race, class, and gender/sexual orientation. We want our students to begin to ask questions not simply of the role of one single aspect of the triad, but rather to question the dynamic at work in the interplay between other, connected parts of the triad. That is to say, rather than asking how race is at work in Richard Wright's *Black Boy*, for instance, students might wonder how the relationship between race *and* class works there, or between race *and* gender—and by looking at the complex dynamic between these two elements, our students are more likely to write about compli-cated interchanges rather than rehearse static assumptions about society. They are also more likely to see how these three aspects of the triad may be interrelated in quite hidden and surprising ways.

Making such connective links possible requires that students discover—and analyze—just what their "natural" position of analysis is in a culture first. We can make this happen by providing our students with a series of difficult questions in relation to the metonyms and cultural events they chose to work with.

- Where do you locate yourself in the triad? What is your ethnicity, class, and race?
- If you have difficulty marking your place in the triad, how might that be signifi-cant? Where do you feel like you fit in, and when don't you?
- How does the way you behave correlate to how you fit or do not fit within the triad?
- Do you feel like you "fit in" when you are interpreting your cultural event or object?
- How does your own interaction with the cultural object or event evidence an intersection of the triad? What might be significant and important to understand about this intersection?
- Does your position in the triad lead you to be proud of the cultural event or object, or do you feel shame about it?
- Can you write about our own placement within the triad without perpetuating the same dynamic of pride or shame? What feels important about your answer to this question?

By asking these questions, and combining a rich discussion of our students' an-swers with examples of writers who ask difficult questions of their own work, we can do much to help them complicate their analyses and deepen an awareness of their methodology, the ways in which their approach can be modified or improved.

We suggest two last questions that students should consider as they begin writing the first drafts of their essays:

- How can you create bridges between related dynamics without reducing them to their essential similarity?
- How can you ask increasingly difficult questions of your paper without it fall-ing apart?

Below, we provide a class-by-class progression of assignments that can lead stu-dents from cultural readings to effective writing about culture, as well as a model student essay that arose from our work in the classroom.

A SAMPLE PROGRESSION FOR ESSAYS ON CULTURE

We begin this progression by reading a collection of essays on different as-pects of culture. In performing these readings, students will look for two or three things at once—they will try to mark the way these writers use metonymy, the way they engage these metonymies in a cultural controversy, and how this writing may be relevant to the concerns of the class.

After students have chosen two of the essays that particularly intrigue them, because of their topics and because they think that their ideas are worth further examination, we will direct them to begin writing creatively about a social issue of political significance, whether or not it initially seems part of their everyday lives. They will research this issue until they can describe it with ease, clarity, and precision.

This essay culminates when students begin listing metonyms for their chosen issues that arise from their own lives. By developing these symbols in narratives and linking them in surprising and effective ways to a social controversy and professional essays, they are positioned to write work that is personally and politically invested. Such work invites the kind of questioning our class employs later in the drafting process, from playing with the idea of a "blind spot" in the analysis to working with new relations in the triad.

The logic of the progression aims to keep the writer continually returning to ideas developed in earlier exercises, questioning them, and building new ideas and new readings out of that recursive action. As a whole, it works to encourage rethinking, symbolic creativity, and effective cultural criticism over the course of 9 class sessions.

PROGRESSION TWO: CULTURE AND ITS POLITICS

Class 1—Introduction to Cultural Issues

Read: Martin Luther King's "Letter from Birmingham Jail" (2000) and an excerpt from René Girard's *Violence and the Sacred* (1977).

Journal: In your journal, list as many of these authors' rhetorical strategies as you can. Then list the particular examples they use to support their wider arguments. Why are they effective or problematic?

Write: Describe three social events that you have attended, that you believe highlight issues of cultural difference, and that hold particular significance for you. These events may be personal in nature—an instance of a family tradition, for example—or public, like a political demonstration, a concert, a church service, or a sporting event. What matters is that you pick events that seem to evoke the problems of cultural difference articulated by King and Girard. We'll discuss these in class. (2 pages)

Class 2

Read: George Orwell's "Marrakech" (2000), Jamaica Kincaid's "On Seeing England for the First Time" (2000), and Toni Morrison's "The Site of Memory" (2000).

Write: Now that you've read three more essays wrestling with the issues surrounding cultural difference, choose one of your events (or decide on a new one) that poses the most interesting thinking problem for you. Write an extended narrative, bringing this event alive for your readers. You should not comment explicitly on the problem, but use the event to evoke it in a detailed manner. (2–3 pages)

continued

PROGRESSION TWO: CULTURE AND ITS POLITICS
(continued)

Class 3
Read: Gloria Anzaldua, "How to Tame a Wild Tongue" (2000) and selections from Judith Butler, *Bodies That Matter*.
Write: Choose one of the essays we've read so far, and write a one- to two-page analysis of the ways their theories help you think through the problem explored in your event. You should think with your author, using his or her theoretical framework to see your event in a new way, but you should also think about the aspects of the problem that their thinking might miss.

CLASS 4
Read: Richard Rodriguez, "The Achievement of Desire" (2000b) and Griselda Pollock's "Feminism/Foucault—Surveillance/Sexuality" (1994).
Journal: Choose a second text from the progression, and respond to it through freewriting. Write about at least three important ideas from this essay or excerpt, that may help you to think through your problem.
Write:
Part One: Think back to the way Kincaid describes her father's hat. Now choose a metonym that you may use to bridge *your own life* with your thinking problem—without mentioning the thinking problem explicitly. This metonymic piece might center on an object, a moment, a memory, or a ritual to which you have a deep personal connection. But at the same time, this object, etc., must evoke the larger problem you're thinking about. You'll exchange this piece with a classmate, who will help you to develop it. (2–3 pages)
Part Two: With the help of your second author, your primary author, and any other evidence you like, respond to your thinking problem with your own provisional theory. Though you needn't draw your metonym into this writing, you should continue to have it in mind. (1 page)

CLASS 5
Read: Philip Brian Harper, selections from *Private Affairs* (1999).
Write:
Part 1: Develop the theory you wrote about last time by speculating on the way that the race/gender/class triad complicates your problem. For instance, consider posing the following questions: How is gender implicated in an author's argument about race? How is an understanding of class essential for understanding what an author is saying about gender? Write two pages of speculative work that complicates your sense of the entangled issues lurking beneath your project.
Part 2: Now take one of your peer's work with metonyms and social issues (Part One of Class Four's writing assignment) and analyze it in two senses—first to help them improve their writing of it, and second to point to new ways they could link their metonyms to their emerging theory. This assignment should run no longer than 1 page.

CLASS 6
Write: In no more than five typewritten pages, do the following three things, but not necessarily in this order:

1. Create a one- to two-page counterargument to your previous theory. In other words, imagine how someone would doubt your theory, and from this new perspective raise good questions and alternative interpretations. Do this in your own voice, within the scope of developing your ideas, employing solid and well-articulated thinking moves.
2. With this new thinking in mind, create another metonym that gestures toward these new ideas. Sweat the details and strive for as vivid a style as possible.
3. Return to the social event with which you began this progression, reflecting on it now through the lens of the new ideas you've developed in your last few exercises.

CLASS 7
Write: Look through the exercises you've written so far and begin to make decisions about which parts are the most important, and which parts you might discard. Begin to imagine the way you might structure the progression of ideas in your essay, and with this structure in mind, revise, combine, and polish two or three of your previous exercises. (4–5 pages)

CLASS 8
Rough drafts due, peer workshopping.

CLASS 9—Paper Due

STUDENT ESSAY

In the following essay by Akiemi Glenn, the controversy over Amadou Diallo's brutal death by New York City police officers is linked to the ritual killing of a boar on Akiemi's family farm. Akiemi begins this progression by drawing us into life on the farm, preparing us subtly and artfully for the connection she finds with the Diallo case. In thinking through her relation to the killing of the boar, Akiemi dives deeply into the work of the anthropologist Rene Girard. It is in the relation between what he calls "sacrifice" or "ritual killing" and social preservation that Akiemi discovers the way that the killing of the boar works metonymically to describe a wider social dynamic. But in making this connection, Akiemi goes further than showing that societies maintain themselves through the ritual killings of scapegoats; rather, she inverts this claim, arguing that in Diallo and the boar, we witness what happens to society when its ritual killings *fail*—when the spectacle of the sacrifice undermines its power to maintain the status quo. This work allows Akiemi to move between critiquing her life on the farm and maintaining a vital political position, without generalization or oversimplification.

When Spectacle Betrays the Sacrifice
by Akiemi Glenn

My sixth Thanksgiving was my first holiday spent in the cold. My immediate family had just relocated East from southern California a few months before and my parents packed us in the van and drove south to North Carolina. My grandparents kept what I figured to be a small petting zoo: a Holstein calf named Cocoa, a coop of chickens, a barn of cats, a few loyal dogs, and a stand of noisy pigs. In the afternoon my father would suit my brother and me up in coats and hats and we would survey the livestock. He would tell us how the rabble the chickens made was the way they talked and showed their love for each other. I thought about the ruckus Grandma made at night when Grandpa tromped his dirty work boots over the floor she had just swept. She must have truly loved him. I always loved a new adventure and this Thanksgiving definitely was one, with the sights and smell of a new country all around me. An adventure I would catalogue and replay over and over till I had it memorized.

My experience that November was the first in a series of incidents that forced me to think about how and why we see ourselves as part of collectives. It forced me to begin to navigate through what was necessity and what was gratuity in our hunger to belong and to cast off, the mercurial urge to draw and re-draw lines, to unite and coalesce around our fears and hopes, and our urge to untie those bonds when they no longer serve us. That November I would be brought to witness an ancient tradition whose strength in building and reinforcing social allegiances also birthed its deepest challenge: A spectacle that undermined the power of tradition.

The day before Thanksgiving, the men of my family assembled in the kitchen of my grandparents' house wearing faces that I would recognize later as belonging to men who are about to go into battle, men who are about to shed blood. They were all there: my father and his three younger brothers, my grandfather and his twin, assorted cousins, all dressed in thick flannel and knitted hats preparing to face the cold. I had no idea what was going on, but I smelled adventure, and I wanted to go with them. I was only six, however, so I had to stay inside with my mother and aunts to start the business of rending a Thanksgiving feast from my grandmother's sparse pantry. I sat with the men while they sloshed down mugs of coffee and inhaled slices of pink bacon pressed between biscuits and then watched them file out the kitchen door and down toward the barnyard, forcing jokes and laughter all the way.

I had been told to stay in the house, but I wanted to be part of any excitement there was. When my mother was busy with my two-year-old brother, who was throwing a fit, I slunk into the guestroom and pulled two blue sweaters, a hat, gloves, and a coat over the clothes I had been wearing. My aunts were in the parlor arguing with my grandmother over the most becoming patterns for her next quilt when I unlatched the kitchen door and followed the sounds of masculine voices to the barn. I crept into the barn and scuttled up into the loft. The men were in the side yard, standing around the pigpen making comments, telling jokes and tall tales. My uncle George claimed that he had seen a deadly Appalachian Horn Snake when he was hunting in the woods and that when it spotted him it tucked the horn at the end of its tail into its mouth and made itself a hoop and rolled after him. Everyone laughed. I did, too, but I held my gloved hands over my mouth to keep my cover.

I could see very little of the pen in the side yard through the slats in the old barn loft, but when the voices died down and trailed off I felt a sharp cold blow across my face. And then I heard the sound that would wake me up that night from a deep sleep and would ring in my ears at the next day's Thanksgiving feast, the sound that would make me sick at meals to come. I saw my father from my hiding place and through the slats I could see that he held a rifle, which he must have brought with him from the house. At the same moment there began a deep, desperate moan that made the whole barn suddenly feel colder. The only people outside were the men I had seen in the kitchen, and my eyes darted to find which of them uttered the sound, but they were all composed, standing, silent. I followed the cry with my eyes and found the big boar in my grandfather's pen backing into a corner with the whites of his big round eyes showing like moons. The moan grew louder and longer. It grew higher, sounding like an infant squealing. The keening swelled and I cupped my hands over my ears to keep it out, but I kept looking. I saw my father raise the rifle and take aim at the boar, who had begun frantically clawing into the frozen ground. There was a loud shot that shook me more than any tremors I had ever felt living on the San Andreas Fault. I looked and there was blood brighter than I had seen in all my six years streaming down between the pig's eyes, now rolling rhythmically back into his fleshy head.

He did not die right away. As he lay writhing, my uncles jumped into the pen and lugged him by his hooves, wailing, to an apparatus attached to the barn. They hoisted him and hooked him through his snout, still crying, and took a long knife and slit his stomach and his veins and let the blood pool in a galvanized tub. His body jerked for a few minutes and he was still, and then his crying stopped.

November is the optimum time for killing, at least that's what my grandfather would tell me at the dinner table several Thanksgivings later. There is something about the cold that makes the blood run quicker out of a cut animal, that makes the death stink less, and makes the screams easier on the ears. When I padded down from the loft only a few minutes later with my ears numbed and reddened from the wind I felt colder than I had ever. I snuck back in through the kitchen and into my room and pulled off layer after layer, determined to keep what I had seen to myself. I ran into my grandmother in the hallway, and I was certain that she knew what I had seen. She sized me up and said, "I know that look, young lady. I can tell by the red in your cheeks what you've been up to." I wanted her to tell me that I had imagined it, that I hadn't witnessed a murder, that my family members wouldn't do that, but then she said, "You were picking through my cookie jar. Well, that's all right. Children should have sweets. Do you want to help me start making the pies for tomorrow?"

So I rolled piecrusts with her all day and that night I went to sleep, but only for a little while. I thought I heard someone screaming and I stayed awake, shivering till morning. At breakfast the family circled the huge table and sat down to a thick meal of grits, sausage, bacon, eggs and black coffee. In my grandmother's kitchen there were two stoves, one with gas burners, one fueled by wood, left over from when the house was renovated in 1910. The wood stove was heated only occasionally; this day it was not. Today it had a head sitting on it, the boar's head, with the mouth wide open, dried blood at the corner contrasting with the rows of white teeth, the sockets sunken where those rolling eyes had been.

My sixth Thanksgiving I did not eat. I spent the evening in the huge guest bed curled up and crying. My mother made the excuse that it was the trauma of moving to a foreign coast, or that I was shy around my newly introduced family members, but she did not know. She couldn't. For years afterward I remembered the boar and his screams of knowing, the terrible noise of mortality.

This scene had been played out before, with different actors; no doubt the men and the boar had been exchanged with the men and a cow, or the men and a goat, the women and a chicken. Death was a fact of farm life. The tilled ground demanded blood sacrifice. The people needed to eat, I was reasoned to, as I recoiled at hunting stories and candied corpses at subsequent holiday tables. The killing was how we survived cold winters in a desperate land. The killing of creatures was how my parents had survived, and theirs. This continual cycle was the only way that I could have ever been conceived. There was, at some point, a necessity to the violence. Survival, in the physical sense, required that human beings eat by any means. My family's survival, in the cultural sense, stipulated that there be ritual killings every November so that we would not forget the hardships of our forebears. We did not slaughter our own, in the strictest sense. There is no mention in the cache of killing-stories of a cousin or a son sliced open so that the other members of the clan could eat, or so that the gods could be appeased. The animals instead died for us, they absorbed the violence that would have otherwise destroyed human lives and with them our attempts to carve out a place in a difficult land.

The victims were always animals, but they were always our animals, the livestock kept in pens, hand fed and named. Enough like us to matter, to be cared for, and enough like us to suffice for us in the symbolic death. According to anthropologist René Girard (1977), this kind of sacrifice does more than express gratitude externally, from humans toward nature. It also serves to ritualize and structure societal violence, the kind of violence that might erupt from interpersonal tensions but is instead channeled into communal, ritual action. For sacrifice "from the animal realm" we choose victims "who were, if we might use the phrase, most human in nature," writes Girard in *Violence and the Sacred*. An animal victim is sought "at the crucial moment to prevent violence from attaining its designated victim" (p. 6). In "primitive" societies when it became apparent that constant eruptions of violence between members of the community would disintegrate social bonds and could jeopardize the existence of the entire group, an outlet for the aggression was sought in socially sanctioned sacrificial violence, as a sort of deferment. But for the sacrifice to be effective the social group needed to find in its victim a balance of similarity and repulsive otherness; they had to be able to both realize and deny that the violence would otherwise be intended for a member of their own community. These rituals from primitive origins function in modern society in ways that are routinely ignored, part of the misunderstanding that ensures the "ability to conceal the displacement upon which the rite is based" (p. 5).

In Western cultures, where physical violence is sublimated, it can be expressed in equally "violent" ways, if only in the aggressive spirit and wish to separate and control individuals. There is a tendency in the West to simultaneously conflate and confuse—and to be confused by—the realities of lived experience in the physical and the lived experience of the mind. As theory increasingly becomes prescriptive in our social interactions and, in so doing, becomes descriptive of them, the seams where theory joins pragmatics show in ways that are at once unrecognizable and spectacular to Western eyes. Thus, we are a society that can pronounce without hesitation a distaste for physical violence but still must create spaces, both rhetorical and literal, for the violence-urge to manifest itself, often shunting it through the absolving filter of "lesser," symbolic, and acceptable vehicles of emotional and intellectual violence. To say this another way, civilizations such as that in the United States have a tendency to deny the power of the psychic on social demands. This means that we must satisfy the needs of ritual violence in much less open and obvious ways than other, so-called primitive, societies. In the West, as Girard describes, there is a constant search to find "a radically new type of violence, truly decisive and self-contained, a form of violence that will put an end once and for all to violence itself" (p. 27). Reactions of outrage to physical violence often mimic the sacrificial as participants try to exorcize the specter of violence. When our judicial system, for example, separates someone off as a "criminal" and symbolically offers him or her up to an ideal of justice, or when a penal system carries out harsh punishments and even kills, we see it as a "less violent," and more final, alternative to the mob violence that Girard describes in primitive societies. The legal machine carries out its frequent and institutionalized sacrifices so modern society will have its tensions eased without having to soil hands with what it fears most: unregulated violence.

But these rituals of the judicial and penal systems do not always satiate the larger group's appetite for sacrifice, and the emotional, symbolic rituals cannot always evenly match the physical in performing atonement.

Tears ran down the face of the woman next to me as we moved south down Fifth Avenue. Thousands of us carried our confusion, homemade signs, and our fear to the streets. One . . . Two . . . Three . . . One woman asked a police officer, one of hundreds decked in riot gear corralling us in like cattle, "What if it were your son? What if it were you shot that many times?" Seventeen . . . Eighteen . . . Nineteen . . . He smirked for a minute and wrapped a wide hand around his billy club.

We counted this time for Amadou Diallo, outraged and hoping that this would be the last time we would have to count the bullets wasted on an unarmed man, hoping that we would not ever have to count the bullets that struck our own loved ones, hoping that we would not be caught in the crossfire of a police mistake. None of the protesters I saw attacked police officers. They chanted, "This is a wallet, not a gun," mocking the four acquitted officers' defense that they thought Diallo was brandishing a pistol when he was only clutching his wallet. The screamed "Murderers!" at the officers who eyed us as if we were ready for a riot. Some of us were. A girl ahead of me spit on an officer who had been riding a scooter beside her. He jumped off and reached into the crowd, pulling her by her hair into the street where he forced her face down and began to fumble with the handcuffs. Other protesters went to help her and he sprayed mace. Policemen eventually subdued him and helped the girl and the blinded protesters back onto the sidewalk.

Briefly violent interactions were interspersed throughout the long walk from Fifty-Ninth Street to City Hall. The police usually initiated it, but the protesters wanted it. They wanted a fight. They wanted the police to club them, to scream back, they wanted proof that the city gave badges and guns to barbarians. It was the only way to reconcile that four men had killed another man, seemingly unprovoked. One of the parties involved had to be less than human, and since we could see ourselves in the vulnerable place of the unarmed Amadou Diallo, the crowd chose the police. Even though these were not the officers who murdered Diallo in a hail of 41 bullets, and these were not the cops who went to trial and were acquitted of all charges, they looked enough like them in their blue uniforms, with their night sticks and guns, to appease the crowd. Lines had been transgressed and were being redrawn. The four policemen who shot Diallo in the Bronx in a single act of physical violence had crossed the line from protectors to predators and this crowd placed the entire NYPD and the city administration on the opposite side of that boundary that separated Them and Us.

Here were two sacrifices working against each other. The first was the killing of Diallo, an otherwise nondescript character among millions in New York City. Diallo became a martyr not for anything he believed in but for what he stood for, most importantly that he stood for us and that in the symbolism of his death we saw our own vulnerabililty. In terms of Girard's analysis of sacrifice, Diallo is the victim who "is sacred only because he [is] killed" (p. 1). And here was the second sacrifice: the people angered by what they considered a miscarriage of justice targeted policemen who had nothing to do with the death, and who probably didn't even know the acquitted officers. These officers were substituted to revive the negative emotions that could have otherwise divided the crowd in violence. The media compared the Diallo verdict to the case of Rodney King in Los Angeles in 1992. They highlighted the fact that the police were native born whites and that Diallo was an immigrant and suggested that New York would riot along racial lines. But the crowd that protested was diverse in age, ethnically, and economically, and stayed cohesive primarily because there was a focus for outrage: the NYPD.

The sacrifice did not need to be literal to be effective. Few people actually would have carried out what some protestors' signs called for, that we "Shoot the Police." The word "Justice" was intoned as though it were some remote entity that demanded the city's admission of guilt and the symbolic sacrifice of the police as a sort of offering to pacify it. The exchange of sacrifice and counter-sacrifice came out of a frightened city; a society that felt its division. The four officers admitted it in their defense testimony. They shot because they feared for their lives. The protesters echoed that same fear when asked why they took to the streets in civil disobedience. Fear is a motivating force in all sacrifice. In religious sacrifice there is the dread of divine retribution if the offering is performed improperly or if it is not made in time to stay the deity's wrath—it is the maintenance of a contract between the people and an idea, a reality that is otherwise intangible to them. In social sacrifice, which happens daily in numerous ways, including the enforcement of laws that sacrifice by punishing individuals for transgressing predetermined rules, there is the specter of social disintegration that must be appeased.

I have been thinking about this cycle, about how sacrifice both tears and repairs the social fabric, since the day that I heard the scream of the boar. I can understand how the experience of ritual sacrifice allows a group to create a semblance of coherence out of some of their most violent and disruptive needs. But I also believe that from a certain angle, or when too much is demanded of it, the transformative action of sacrifice is interrupted, and its effect is more divisive than cohesive. Sacrifice exists because it is perceived to repair some damage to the social fabric. Humans apparently found no necessity in sacrifice, or in curbing their violence, until they found necessity in maintaining the social order. It continues to have a necessity, just as the slaughter of the boar functioned as a reminder and as a practical means of survival, just as the protest allowed frustrations to be dissipated. At the core of every symbolic sacrifice there is an origin in physical necessity. In the sacrifice of the boar there was the history of people living brutish lives and killing to survive. It was necessary to eat to live.

But the sacrifice can be undermined by its own spectacular nature. Sitting in the freezing loft of my grandparents' rickety barn watching my family members slice through the flesh of the old boar, I was less impressed with the "necessity" of the scene and more with the visual image of it, the blood, the obvious pain of the victim, his terrible voice. These things gave the scene power, but they also drove me outside the circle of my family, causing me to skip the ritual dinner, to begin to interrogate it and other traditions with questions and doubt on subsequent Thanksgiving. Similarly, the anonymity of the police uniforms, and especially the intimidation of their riot gear, made it easy to scapegoat them as other, as the enemy; the spectacle of their power actually imbued the scene with power. This process allowed the crowd to experience their anger and fear in, ultimately, what seemed a safe way. But it is also necessary to recognize the risk in this second sacrifice and the way that the spectacle of the relatively powerless sacrificing the powerful presents more than the simple problem of cohesion versus disintegration. This second sacrifice threatens a society that is not only a mass to be unified or divided, but is also stratified as a hierarchy of authority and submission. The spectacular nature of this set-up is apparent when its base—the old societal problem of unification versus division—begins to rock.

The ostensible objective of sacrifice is to remove the individual who challenges the group's cohesion or to defer the blame for disintegration on another party. In practice, however, it also eradicates the victim's agency, and consigns them to silence. If the purpose of sacrifice is to teach tradition and to establish allegiance with the dominant social order it failed with me in both experiences. The grotesque spectacle repulsed me from any identification with the culture of the sacrifice. I neither felt safe with a family that shed blood to fill plates nor in a city patrolled by hair-trigger policemen. It is excess that transforms an act into a spectacle; it was the horror of the pig's violent death that I remembered and the horror of the force used in Diallo's murder that drew New Yorkers to the streets. Because they are brief and forcefully imbued with emotion it is, to some degree, this identification that reinstates the victim's agency after death, if only in the understanding of observers, by drawing attention to the absence of the victim's vocalization. It was after his death that the pig's voice had the most power. My brother and I had visited his pen, but his everyday grunts did not keep me up at night. I had patted his bulbous head as we made our rounds in the barnyard but it was not until it sat leering at me in the kitchen that it spoke the loudest. Diallo, whose voice I never heard, rang through the streets with every syllable chanting for justice.

The victims, though weak and outnumbered in the sacrifice, do not ever fully relinquish agency as long as there are observers outside the sacrifice who hear the voice, who recognize the spectacle and feel its power, who perceive the victims as more than pawns in a rational system for easing social tensions. Entertainment of the irrational—that a man can speak beyond the grave, that a pig can speak at all—is a means for sacrifice, however inevitable, to be overcome, and for its silence to be filled. In this way, when sacrifice goes too far, when it becomes extreme in its violence, or imprudent in its frequency, it undermines itself. Though the patterns of sacrifice may spiral out ad infinitum, the patterns are sometimes interrupted and checked by a disjuncture—when agency is inadvertently given to the weak, the sacrifice will fail.

WORK CITED

Girard, R. (1977). *Violence and the sacred*. Baltimore: Johns Hopkins.

8 *Thinking and Writing with Popular Culture*

> Culture is ordinary, and the ordinary is highly significant.
>
> —John Fiske

In the first chapter of this book, we critiqued some teachers' tendency to blame students' passivity in the classroom on their participation in a culture of consumption, claiming that this scapegoating covers over a deeper problem: the difficulty of figuring out what good thinking is and how it can be taught. Throughout these chapters, we've argued that teaching effective writing begins with recognizing the forms in which students already think. If this is the case, then we shouldn't simply scapegoat consumer culture as an insuperable barrier to rich intellectual work. Rather, given that shopping, instant messaging, channel and web surfing, watching television and movies—technological and cultural forms—shape and structure our students' lives, we should find ways to use them as content in the writing classroom.

The impulse to use popular culture in academic settings is far from new. In fact, the very forms of popular culture that we in the university like to blame for our students' "failures" have themselves served as objects of study throughout academia for years. By the time postmodernism rolled through the university, "low" culture had become a popular topic of study within the various wings of the liberal arts. From the Frankfurt school forward, scholars have been reading canonical texts against popular ones, investigating the society pages in magazines with methods previously reserved for Hemingway and Faulkner, analyzing advertisements with the serious thought once reserved for Mondrian, and interpreting cartoon sketches alongside Lichenstein paintings. And those methods, and that "serious thought," have not been untouched by these "low-brow" objects of study; new thinking methods, and paradigm-shifting ways of understanding, have developed out of this work with popular culture.

One such shift in method, important to our work in the classroom, is an emphasis on analyzing the ways in which subtle forces of power produce and govern the behavior of subjects. It's obvious that structures like school systems, governments, churches, and families "transmit values" to us, forcefully influencing our beliefs about the world. The productions and technologies of popular culture do the same. Many scholars have shown how cultural productions create and maintain ideologies that benefit the status quo by providing us with "pictures of the world and our place in it," as James Kavanaugh (1996) puts it, delineating the difference between "proper" and "improper" behavior, and between what we should take pleasure in and what we should not. At the same time, scholars have shown the ways in which pop culture often purposefully (or unconsciously) critiques and subverts dominant power structures, opening up spaces for new ways of thinking and living.

This double action of popular culture—the way it enforces and undermines social norms at the same time—makes it a content area ready-made for work in the classroom. In that enforcing and undermining is already a double movement, a dialectical action. If we can lead students to recognize the way they are implicated in this double action through their own desires and resistance, we've led them to a space where thinking can thrive.

READING STUDENTS' RELATION TO POPULAR CULTURE

There are two default positions to which students commonly resort when they are asked to write about popular culture: praise and blame. Ask them to choose and critique a song, television show, music video, or scene from a film that intrigues them, and they tend to choose something that they love and write an encomium to it. Or they pick something that is easy for them to despise, and wind up criticizing those who like it, judging "herd behavior" rather than marking their own problematic relation to it. These initial judgments are too easy, but once identified, they can provide beginning places from which to push writers toward the work of reflection and dialectical thinking.

Writers can learn best to write about popular culture through recognizing what their "natural" positions of enjoyment and criticism look like—that is to say, when they recognize the ways in which they enjoy and critique popular culture in their everyday lives. Once they do, we can use these default positions to train them to enact new, more challenging forms of analysis. To do this, we will have some fun bringing our students' favorite pop cultural objects into the classroom—and our job, initially, is to take pleasure in these objects, for if we're not involved in enjoyment, the dialectics cannot begin. We ask our students to choose movies, advertisements, television shows, music, popular books, Internet sites, or any other piece of cultural production they want, and begin talking, thinking, and writing about them. To help our students determine their "natural" position of analysis, we ask them to identify for themselves just which aspects of these objects fascinate them. By drawing our students' genuine tastes into the space of the classroom, then, and by evoking their involvement, we avoid the problem of students writing cynical narratives about the idiocy of someone else's favorite (and problematic) desires, as represented by the cultural productions "those people" enjoy. Then, by helping them to critique the objects with which they've chosen to work, and their relation to those objects, we'll avoid, in turn, essays written from the point of view of the fanatic.

Just as our students learned to discover artworks that fascinated them and gave rise to the kinds of complexities, paradoxes, and ambiguities that open a space for successful thinking, so, too, can they learn to locate those instances of pop culture that move them. Being moved by popular culture almost always entails some sort of negotiation and revision of a socially contested value, for it is impossible to enjoy *anything* without becoming involved, whether consciously or not, with some issue that matters. Teachers can make the process of thinking deeply about popular culture less abstract by showing students how to find a suitable site for contestation in what matters to them. The kinds of controversies that make for effective writing can be discovered by means of our students' own experience of the dialectic between enjoyment and critique, between fascination and repulsion.

Such work in the writing classroom is first based on identifying what we experience everyday, or "what we have." Finding the best examples to work with, then, sometimes entails finding that thing that represents a negotiation between an old value and a new one, or that engages us in the place our consciously articulated values come into conflict with our secret desires.

We are drawn to certain aspects of popular culture for often contradictory reasons, and contradictions then provide a springboard for thinking. Classroom exercises can train students to find the kinds of cultural contradictions that provide thinking problems worth pursuing. Below are a few of the prompts for freewriting that we use to help them develop ways of choosing and examining relationships between cultural productions and their desire:

- Describe an object that represents a way that your tastes "collide" with someone else's taste. Is there something that you genuinely like that other people genuinely dislike? Could this be more than a matter of taste? What do you think is being contested in terms of the object itself? What is contested by the contradictory interpretations (celebration, critique) that you and this other person have?
- Imagine that you stole something as a child that you no longer want owing to your political or social beliefs. Write about taking it back: What would you say to the clerk, the owner of the business, the maker of the thing that you've stolen? What do you think they would say to you?
- In the satirical newspaper *The Onion*, an article featured a man who claimed that he only purchased Diet Coke because it "resonated with his image" and not because he was thirsty. Obviously, *The Onion* is poking fun at how effective marketing is in the psychological lives of everyday people. What experiences with marketing do you have, that either confirm the suspicions of *The Onion*, or seem to undermine them?
- Think of your favorite television show. Now explain why you like it. Explain who you are as a member of a demographic. What are the issues that the show explores? Does it stumble on problems it never intended to—and do these problems seem to stem from your own particular community of belief? What genre does your show belong to? How is it changing the genre it exists in? What is different here? Does that difference matter? What is at stake in your interpretation—what turns on it?

We use discussion about these early writings to outline some basic dynamics—ways that popular culture works through contradiction and paradox. Such thinking, and the range of examples we hear in the classroom at this time, provides a foundation for students to think broadly about popular culture in general. As we did in the visual arts progression, we want our students to begin by trafficking in excess: to work across many pop cultural productions, finding connections and disjunctions across genres, tests, and events. We'll ask them to keep track of the broad trends that they notice as they narrow their focus and construct close readings of individual objects; by working back and forth between particular examples and the range of productions they're interested in, they can develop arguments that are both complex and important. And as they move from this "excessive" work toward choosing their particular pieces of pop culture evidence, their foundational work should help them to know the value of choosing productions to which they are drawn, and by which they are repulsed at the same time; the more complex their viewing/listening/consuming relation to the piece of cultural production, the more fruitful their thinking about it will be.

A SCHEMA FOR FLEXIBLE CRITIQUE

In the spirit of our earlier work with metonymy, once our students have explored a broad range of pop culture productions, we push them toward focusing on a condensed example—an image, event, or moment that speaks to larger issues. Once students have found a suitable object for analysis, interrogated their enjoyment of and resistance to the object, and thought carefully about the diverse ways such a packed example can be interpreted, they will be ready to speculate on how that item may be related to the wider culture in which it exists.

While leading students to do this interpretive work, teachers need to be careful to bracket our own beliefs, opening up spaces in which students can think independently. It should not surprise us that we have our own default modes for thinking about popular culture—whether that is as intellectuals writing from a theoretical perspective, or as participants in our everyday world of entertainment and big media. If we do not recognize this fact, we may be in danger of foisting our own critical methods onto our students, whether or not those methods are the best for the wide range of viewpoints and experiences represented by the students in our classes. In other words, we may inadvertently fetishize our perspective by employing it in every example we choose, "teaching" our students how to think about popular culture the way we ourselves do.

Instead, we need to articulate frameworks that allow students to approach cultural objects from radically different angles than those we might take as thinkers.

Let's imagine that one of our students has decided to focus on the video for Jennifer Lopez's (2002) hit song "Jenny From the Block." Wisely, our student initially chose the video because of his own contradictory relation to it. A feminist, this student wanted to criticize J. Lo as an artist because he believed that she uses her body to sell her music and her image. As a Latino, he feels that she's a sellout, imitating the white images of power and wealth that have until now excluded Latinas from superstardom. But once he begins watching the video, he finds himself surreptitiously taking pleasure in it, because of the way the camera sets up her body for viewing pleasure. This implication in the logic of the video raises some questions for him, about feminism, fetishism, consumerism, class, and race, among other things. This good start is what the student brings to class. It occasions an opportunity time to introduce a thinking structure that will push him to complicate his reading without overdetermining the content of his analysis.

We would ask the student, and everyone in the class, to push beyond their initial questions by working on at least one other axis of this triad:

Pop Culture Object or Event

Creator   Audience
(production)   (reception)

We draw this triad on the board and then ask the writers in the class to locate which of the three areas they have focused on so far in their thinking about their chosen object; likely, because of the work we've done already, most of them will have focused on the reception angle—themselves. We want them to focus not on one node, but on the dynamics that exist between them, so once students have thought about another point on the triad, we'll ask them to think *between* two or more.

In class, by focusing on the "Creator/Object" relationship in the video, the student might realize that there is some tension between the lyrics of J. Lo's song and the images the director has chosen, as well as the way she performs herself in those images. The lyrics argue for her hip-hop authenticity, directing her listeners to disregard her diamonds and to remember her roots as a South Bronx native.

The video's images, however, do not position J. Lo in her neighborhood, or with people from that neighborhood—and certainly not as she looked when she was in that neighborhood. Images locate her shopping for a jeweled watch, being photographed at a fashion shoot, standing at the window of a luxury hotel, sunbathing on a yacht with her (not from the South Bronx) fiancé, Ben Affleck—these are classic celebrity images. But these images are also shot with some irony—they are partially obscured, blurry, the way paraparrazi shots usually are, as if the images are giving us J. Lo only through the eyes of the media.

The plot thickens. Our student, having examined the object carefully in its own right, might have to question the creator's intentions—both the director's, and J. Lo's choices in how she presents herself as an artist. He should wonder if the video is attempting to implicate him in the desires he thought were constructed outside of him, by providing the kind of voyeuristic views that can trap him into enjoying a piece of popular culture he would, in a thinking moment, dismiss. Her lyric "don't be fooled" now takes on new meaning, after some consideration of the way the video is shot. He might wonder: Is she hinting to us not to be fooled by the video itself, and by the images of her that the media constantly sells us?

Once our student begins thinking through the three points on the triangle, he may admit that much of the contradictory effect of the video is probably intentional. Then the question is if the pleasure it offers doesn't serve to undermine this intended critique. By extension, he should think through what this teaches him about his own pleasure, and his own feminism.

Our student has now gone through a complex process in examining the three points of the triad. He's begun to identify themes in the video, noting which develop because of explicit message and visual images, among other things. And he's connected these formal elements to consideration of the context that surrounds the object itself—both on the side of production (the director's vision, J. Lo's negotiation with self-representation) and reception (his own warring beliefs and desires). If we can take our students through this work of noting form and content in the object itself, while drawing connections between those structures and messages and the contexts in which the object functions, we can draw all of our students to make these discoveries for themselves.

We often perform model work like this in the classroom, with particularly rich cultural productions like the video. Then we ask our students to go home and consider their chosen piece of pop culture through this process. By invoking two of the nodes of the triad, our students become engaged in a complex interaction, not only between their chosen site and its implications, but with a dynamic the implications of which are even more telling for an intellectual analysis of the chosen object.

Here are some questions that can push students to think through the three sides of the triangle we've given them:

1. Creator and Object: What are the convergences or tensions between the goals of the artist or company and the products they create? What are the overt, and covert, values it seems that the creator has? How are these values manifested in, and undermined by, the form and/or content of the object?
2. Object and Audience: What are the "hidden agendas" of the object? What does the object leave unsaid? What is assumed about the audience, in the way the object is produced and sold? What common desires, fantasies, etc. is the object positioned to fuel and/or fulfill?
3. Audience and Artist: How does the audience see a symbol in the daily struggle of the artist herself? In this case, students ask questions about convergences and dissimilarities between their own lives and the biographical life of the artist, looking for relationships they both share as mutual participants in a culture. What implications does an artist's betrayal or celebration of her own community mean to her audience(s)?

A SAMPLE PROGRESSION FOR ESSAYS ON POPULAR CULTURE

We begin this progression by reading a collection of essays on different aspects of popular culture. We also watch a *Frontline* episode called "Merchants of Cool," which provides a springboard into discussing the issues surrounding the marketing of "cool culture" to youth in the United States. Students choose one of the essays that particularly intrigues them, because of its topic and because they think that its ideas are worth further examination. With this essay's ideas as their main ally, they begin to collect other pieces of evidence—pieces of popular culture (advertisements, films, television programs, and commercials, etc.) and at least two other written texts that help them to set up a thinking problem and analyze it. This work culminates in an essay in which they evaluate their central thinker's ideas against their own thinking, the piece(s) of popular culture they've examined, and a social controversy that is deepened as a result of this thinking.

The logic of the progression is to keep the writer continually returning to ideas developed in earlier exercises, questioning them, and building new ideas and new readings out of that recursive action. It's meant to encourage rethinking and rereading, and in the process allow students to draft essay parts early in the process so they can begin the work of finding the best shape for their essay as they're coming up with their ideas. The structure of the progression also encourages a movement back and forth between focusing on individual cultural objects and drawing connections between many pieces of evidence. If they work through the exercises, it's hard for a student to make it through this progression without recognizing and questioning their default modes of interpretation, and complicating their initial thinking about the way popular culture and culture in general interact.

PROGRESSION THREE: THE GRAMMAR OF POPULAR CULTURE

CLASS 1
Read: John Fiske, "Popular Culture" (1996); Gladwell, "The Coolhunt" (1997); and Paul Fussell, "Indy" (2000).
Journal: Write a paragraph each for five pieces of pop culture that intrigue you. Your brief descriptions should highlight the way that these pieces present contradictions and inspire questions. You should also begin to identify and analyze your own personal relation to the events and images in question. Finally, consider alternative ways of thinking through your examples, looking for surprising, creative angles for inquiry.

CLASS 2
Read: Slavoj Zizek, "The Matrix, or, Two Sides of Perversion" (2000); Margaret Talbot, "Les Tres Riche Heurs de Martha Stewart" (2000); and Adorno and Horkheimer, "The Culture Industry" (1997).
Journal: Choose the essay you want to use as your primary ally in thinking through popular culture. List four or five ideas from the essay that you want to keep thinking about. Then analyze your thinker's writing style—what kinds of thinking moves does he/she make that you find powerful? What approaches or techniques does the author employ that give you new ideas for approaching your own topic? In your journal, write about one or two thinking moves that the author employs—copy down the sentences in which the writer makes the move, and name it and describe it. Bring your journal to class so you can teach us the move. And use this thinking move in your exercise.
Write: One page summarizing your essay's theory as you understand it so far. Then, in two more pages of work, write about three of your five pieces of pop culture (the same and/or new pieces) through the lens of that theory. What does the theory help you to see about each piece? What does it miss?

CLASS 3
Read: Nietzsche, "On Truth and Lying in an Non-Moral Sense" (1999).
Write: Draft a part of your essay in which you do three things (not necessarily in this order):

1. Choose one of your five pieces of pop culture—ideally, the one that poses the most intriguing problem when you think about it through the lens of your thinker's ideas. Give a sustained description of it and articulate a thinking problem it raises.
2. Consider two more pieces of popular culture that help you to develop provisional theories in response to your problem, analyzing them in terms of their creation, marketing, use, and so on.

(continued)

PROGRESSION THREE: THE GRAMMAR OF POPULAR CULTURE
(continued)

3. Borrow and build on the thinker's ideas to develop a provisional theory about your thinking problem.

Organize this draft part around at least three good thinking moves. At least three pages, typed and double-spaced, please, with a Works Cited page.

CLASS 4

Research: Find any information that will help you be more authoritative about the phenomenon you're analyzing (statistics, context, web site copy advertising your product, etc.), read another essay in your anthology, watch another movie, etc. Use your journal to keep track of new ideas and emerging questions and connections.

Write: Draft a part of your essay in which you do at least three of the following things, using all the written and pop culture evidence you can muster:

1. That provisional theory you developed in your last exercise? Transcend it! Develop another, better theory by interpreting the pop culture evidence you've already written about, but in a new way. But build this theory on the last one, showing how it adds to or disagrees with what you were saying before.
2. Provide a series of other possible theories, using ideas from other critics and examples from new pieces of pop culture.
3. Analyze the kinds of thinking moves your thinker tends to make, in order to argue that his or her theories/ways of thinking are limited; argue for a better way of thinking.
4. Admit to your own involvement in the thinking problem, using a story from personal experience (could be concerning a totally different realm of pop culture than what you're writing about, or not concerning pop culture at all) to complicate a position you've taken. From your own perspective, what can you teach us about why people get caught up in the problem you're writing about?

Organize this draft part around at least three good thinking moves. At least three pages, typed and double-spaced, please. And a Works Cited page.

CLASS 5

Research Suggestions: Reread, rewatch, rethink. Read two exemplary student essays in a handout, "Girls Watching the Media" and "Instant Karma."

Writing: Draft a third part of your essay in which you do at least three of the following things, using all the written and pop culture evidence you can muster:

1. That theory you developed in your last exercise that disagreed with or complicated your original theory? Transcend it! Develop a third way of thinking about things that uses the good elements from both theories and avoids the problems of both, too.
2. Return to a bunch of the pieces of pop culture you've written about so far, articulating new connections and ideas about what they mean to you now, and what you think they should mean for your readers.

3. Introduce a new piece of evidence that destroys everything you've said so far—the piece of pop culture that is the exception to the rule, or the idea from an essay that blows all your thinking away.
4. Articulate a better thinking problem than the one you initially proposed. Argue for why it's better.
5. Articulate all the important questions left unanswered by your writing so far.
6. Return to your thinker, evaluating a new idea from his or her essay that helps to provide a better theory about your problem, or questioning an idea you've agreed with so far.

Organize writing around at least three good thinking moves. At least three pages, typed and double-spaced, please.

CLASS 6
Remember: Bring two copies of your rough draft to class, unless you've volunteered to have your draft read by everyone, in which case you should bring 16 copies.

CLASS 7
Rough Draft Workshop: Peer Editing

CLASS 8
Final draft due.

STUDENT ESSAY

In the following student essay, Alexander Obercian links a wide range of evidence by a tightly constructed series of thinking moves. Alex began this progression by focusing on Shoes of the Fisherman, a brand of sandal produced by a conservative evangelical Christian company. In thinking through the way this product was produced and what its audience must believe in order to buy "Christian" sandals that are designed to witness to unbelievers, Alex began to make some surprising connections. He chose Nietzsche as the thinker he wanted to work with, and began discussing the issues surrounding the "sacred text" being debated after the Columbine shootings. Midway through the progression, we found he was critiquing the beliefs and values underlying these Christian products without enough engagement and complication, so we pushed him to bring a secular product that he purchases into the mix, to compare and contrast with the Christian product. It is in the dialectical movement between Christian and secular advertising techniques, and the beliefs that produce them and are produced by them, that the central question of his essay begins to emerge: If the religious treatment of sacred language and the secular treatment of advertising language are so similar, what does that tell us about what is at stake in the commodification of language? With the help of some smart work with Nietzsche, he proposes that what's at stake in this commodification is truth itself. He ends with a smart "drawing-the-line" move: truth is always constructed, but when we commodify words by treating them as magical, we always sacrifice something.

Instant Karma
by Alexander Obercian

On the morning of April 20, 1999, Eric Harris and Dylan Klebold approach Columbine High school, in Jefferson County, Colorado. Armed with one 10-shot Hi-Point model 995 carbine rifle, one Intratec Ab-10 (TEC-9) pistol, two Savage 12-gauge shotguns, and as many as ninety-five explosive devices, Harris and Klebold enter the school near the cafeteria. Upon doing so, they are met with the words that God commanded unto Moses on Mount Sinai: Thou Shalt Not Kill. Harris and Klebold tremble in fear and shame for what they have come to accomplish. Dropping their weapons, the boys fall to their knees bow their heads in penance, and pray to God for forgiveness.

If only it were that easy. In reality, the boys fired an estimated 900 rounds into the bodies of their fellow classmates, teachers, and eventually, themselves. It is doubtful that the killers knew their bullets would also become ammunition for the Christian Right's agenda. But the seemingly unchecked anathema of school violence is now a selling point in a campaign to legislate morality, and the killing at Columbine is exhibit A. As ridiculous as it sounds to some that Harris and Klebold would suddenly abandon such murderous thoughts, some members of the Christian Right believe that the power of the Word is so inescapable and forceful that even the most vile intentions can be instantly quelled by one glance at the Ten Commandments.

House Majority Whip Tom DeLay would be the first to install a copy of the Ten Commandments in our local schools. He himself believes that the Word would have felled Harris and Klebold: "I got an e-mail this morning that said it all. A student writes, 'Dear God: Why didn't you stop the shootings at Columbine?' And God answers, 'Dear student: I would have, but I wasn't allowed in school'" (Christianity.about.com). The logical assumption to make is that having God in school (in the form of the Ten Commandments) would have prevented Columbine. That is quite a substantial claim, but it only shows the magnitude of faith that some Christians place in the Word.

In 1990, an attempt to pass a law mandating the display of the Ten Commandments in public schools (not coincidentally attached to a gun-control bill) failed for reasons stated by People for the American Way on their website:

> First, posting the Ten Commandments is a solution in search of a non-existent problem. Religious Right rhetoric notwithstanding, religion and prayer have not been banned from public schools; in fact the First Amendment protects students' rights to pray, discuss religious views, and read religious texts in school. Second, posting the Ten Commandments would violate the First Amendment by requiring schools to favor one religion over another; the Supreme Court ruled so in 1980.

What is at stake here is not a student's right to practice religion in school—that right is already guaranteed; rather, the Christian right wants to be seen as doing something about school violence. The Ten Commandments as touted by Tom DeLay become a symbol of spirituality, a means to gauge both the morality of a school population and the proactiveness of the Christian Right in combating school violence.

Not all in the Christian Right are so naïve as to think that the displaying of the Ten Commandments is a panacea for all of society's ills. Yet, no matter to what degree one believes that the Word of God is effective in influencing the casual observer, the shared assumption remains that the Word can somehow change lives. Consider Shoes of the Fisherman beach sandals, one of a myriad of Christian products that touts its divine blessing. An appealing ocean-teal color and, by all accounts on the manufacturer's website, of sturdy construction, these sandals would appear normal enough. However, the soles are alternately etched with the words "Jesus" and "Loves You," the idea being that a stroll on the beach will leave imprints in the sand that will likewise imprint any wayward soul who should happen to gaze upon these divine footprints.

The wearing of these sandals or the displaying of the Ten Commandments in school rests on the belief that spirituality can be imparted instantly, that the power of the Word is so overwhelming that the mere mention of it can lead not just to inspiration, but to salvation. The personal story of Dr. Kathleen Farrell, the President of Shoes of the Fisherman, Inc., continues the ramifications of this belief, displayed on the company's website:

> In college, she was abducted by a stranger. During her captivity, without thinking about what she was saying, she repeated the 23rd Psalm out loud. Praise the Lord, she was released. How important were the words of the Psalm? Kathleen believes they saved her life and perhaps saved the soul of her abductor.

Dr. Farrell, too, wants to lend a hand in preventing school violence: "After the Columbine school tragedy, legislation was proposed to post the Ten Commandments in public places because Biblical reminders can make the difference between life and death" ("Fisherman"). Farrell, like Tom DeLay and others in the Christian Right, want to use Columbine to sell an agenda. The very word "Columbine" creates an anxiety in people that the Christian Right then quells through some form of legislation (Ten Commandments) or product (Shoes of the Fisherman). Before the Christian Right can use the power of the Word to prevent school violence, it must first use the power of Columbine to sell the Word.

Columbine, then, has become a commodity in itself. It is free advertising—one can use it to advance all sorts of agendas, from gun control to censorship to Christian morals. Like the words of the Ten Commandments, the word "Columbine" is meant to impart instant meaning. Immediately one can associate it with everything from the Goth subculture to the downfall of society. Due to the almost incessant use by the media of the school shooting as a byword for societal ills, "Columbine" has been transformed to include a range of meaning greater than the actual physical and historical reality of the shooting itself. The Columbine Research Task Force, a group that is diligently fighting the "commodification" of the shooting, makes this claim:

> We're seeing more of a peripheral grasp of the event—the shooting is used as a catapult to propel other stories deployed by the media; for instance, stories involving gun regulation, or video game violence. The actual shooting becomes a secondary element, and not the main focus.

Where Columbine is presented as a symptom of the problem, the Ten Commandments are presented as the solution. Are not then the Ten Commandments likewise commodified?

Charles Henderson, a Presbyterian minister, agrees that Christianity has a place in public schools, but disagrees with the way the Christian Right has handled the Ten Commandments issue. Henderson argues that the Christian Right is only using the Ten Commandments as a symbol of Christianity. Referring to Tom DeLay's earlier statement about Columbine, Henderson, in an article posted on his website, has this to say:

> Albeit, the Congressman is speaking informally here, but still, his literalism is appalling. Does he seriously believe that by some act of the Congress God might actually be kicked out of our schools? Congressman, you don't have THAT much power!

DeLay and others would seem to presume that by some divine magic the display of the Ten Commandments would actually symbolize a very real increase in the spirituality of the student body. Because the Christian Right presents the Word of God as an antidote for all of society's ills, in commodifying those ills (i.e. Columbine) to sell the Word, the Christian Right is forced to commodify the Word itself.

The commodification of the religious and the secular presents a clever means of advancing one's own agenda. What makes the commodification and associations attached to Columbine or the Ten Commandments so effective in imparting meaning and thus influencing others lies written in the sand—not metaphorically, but literally.

Shoes of the Fisherman understands the power that words have beyond their immediate literal translation. Though we in the secular world may find it ridiculous that a pair of sandals could save somebody's life, secular marketing works in a similar way to Christian marketing. Consider Teva, makers of secular sandals that, if anything, only leave their brand name imprinted on the sand. Teva is explicit as to what each of its sandals "says." Take, for instance, the Sidewalk sandal as described on the company's website:

> These sandals are ready to travel, socialize, talk the talk and walk the walk. They're for people who like to take the less beaten path, but doesn't [sic] need to go where no man has gone before. Casual elegance meets contemporary design.

Teva conveniently eliminated the need for guesswork—no more worrying about buying the wrong pair of sandals. Teva assumes that its customers are minutely aware of their image, and so Teva sells a mind-boggling variety of products, the supposition being that there is a right sandal for everyone, for every "individual."

Teva sandals are effective in transmitting an image because those who buy the sandals and those in the general public who see the sandals being worn have constructed a similar if not identical idea about the role of clothing in determining personal identity. Clothes "speak" about the person wearing them; there is meaning bound up in the clothing. In just the same way, as a result of thorough conditioning by the media and politicians, the general public has begun to find new significance to Columbine. DeLay and the Christian Right are pushing the associations.

Many have confused the image with the reality. A pair of sandals, nothing more than bits of leather and plastic with no inherent meaning, becomes much more. In his essay "On Truth and Lying in a Non-Moral Sense," Nietzsche (1999) describes how such a process occurs:

> What, then, is truth? A mobile army of metaphors, metonymies, anthropomorphisms, in short a sum of human relations which have been subjected to poetic and rhetorical intensification, translation, and decoration, and which, after they have been in use for a long time, strike a people as firmly established, canonical, and binding . . . (p. 146)

We tend to forget that sandals do not possess an inherent essence that speaks to us and to others: "Don't I emanate a cool sophistication?" But as Nietzsche says, this misconception becomes fact through linguistic transformations, and constant use. Advertisers so consistently tout the idea that image is everything that it becomes everything. The catch phrase becomes so ingrained in the capitalist psyche that it becomes dogma. It then seems perfectly reasonable that my individual character could be encapsulated in a pair of mass-produced sandals. "That's right," I say to myself, "I don't take the beaten path. And my sandals prove it!"

Likewise, a member of the Christian Right might find it perfectly reasonable that a pair of sandals, due to the words printed on the soles, could contain some inherent Godlike or divine power capable of saving lives. The same is true of the Ten Commandments—which contain so much meaning and so much power that one look at them could dissuade a murderer.

But what would appear to be inherent in an object is actually created by us. A pair of Teva sandals can only say what the advertising team hired to market them arbitrarily assigns them to say. Similarly, the words Jesus Loves You only save lives because humans have endowed them with divine power. We create a system of contexts and truths in order to relate to the world, but we often remain oblivious to what we have created. So a person wearing a pair of Tevas forgets that the truth that would say his sandals emanate some inherent coolness, is actually a truth created and accepted by himself. As Nietzsche says:

> If someone hides something behind a bush, looks for it in the same place and finds it there, his seeking and finding is nothing much to boast about; but this is exactly how things are as far as the seeking and finding of "truth" within the territory of reason in concerned. If I create the definition of mammal and then, having inspected a camel, declare, "Behold, a mammal", then a truth has certainly been brought to light, but it is of limited value. (p. 147)

The truth often remains of limited value because it is constructed. Furthermore, the truth is only true for those who buy into the system (whether it be Christianity or consumerism) that generates it.

Even if the Jesus Loves You sandals do not save lives, as the website claims, they at least make apparent the folly of such secular modes of commodity fetishism. The same person who believes that Teva sandals are an adequate representation of himself may scoff in the face of Jesus sandals. They would do so only because they have not been sold on the idea that God speaks through products. That God is inherent in commodities is not a part of the system of constructed "metaphors [and] metonymies" that constitute the general version of secular truth. That a person's individual characteristics can be inherent in a pair of sandals, on the other hand, is a part of this truth, and so no right minded capitalist consumer would ever laugh at a Teva advertisement.

Return to Columbine and we see that the analogous meanings that the word Columbine has picked up are also a part of secular truth. Some, like the Columbine Research Task Force, have executed the difficult task of breaking from this truth. The Christian Right, though it has always operated on a different standard of what that truth is, nonetheless has constructed a system for establishing what is true to them. When these truths, the secular and the religious, collide, we can see more clearly the arbitrary nature of both systems. It is by laughing at the absurdity of Jesus sandals that the absurdity of the secular truth is revealed.

Though some of the similarities between Christian and secular commodities may be surprising, it is certainly no revelation that truth is constructed. However, some truths are better than others. As we have seen in the case of Columbine, when an object becomes a commodity, its original meaning is often obscured. Commodification becomes dangerous when that original but obscured meaning continues to carry a power of its own that has the potential to harm or create lasting confusion. Returning to the question of the Ten Commandments and the minister Charles Henderson, we can see such a case.

As Henderson and other critics of the Ten Commandments issue have noted, when the Commandments are viewed for what they really are, and what they really say (as opposed to what they imply about the pervasiveness of the Christian Right) very real practical concerns arise:

> When a school administrator schedules a sporting event on the Sabbath, doesn't that make a mockery of Sabbath observance? Do we intend, by placing such words on a wall, to go ahead and do what the commandments command? And cancel that soccer game? And if so, which Sabbath do our school administrators honor, Saturday or Sunday? (website)

The Christian Right has only dealt with the issue in general terms; specifics such as those raised by Henderson have not been considered. After all, if they examined the text itelf, they would discover many problems related to practical application of the inherent commands. But there is a more serious problem with certain kinds of commodification. The Ten Commandments are not a pair of sandals. They have already a serious historical reality; they carry both weight and meaning. When that meaning is distorted through commodification for political and social purposes, serious consequences can follow. The Christian Right seems to be adept at turning that historical weight and meaning to new ends—ends that threaten the separation between church and state. Commodification permits the Christian Right the over-reaching power to subvert the law.

In attempting to attain this power, members of the Christian Right sacrifice the religious for the political. In the same manner, the students who suffered their end at Columbine are again sacrificed when their deaths become secondary to the political and social significance of the word "Columbine". Sacrifice is inherent in commodities—when a commodity assumes the very identity that makes it a commodity, it necessarily sacrifices inherent or original content. In the case of sandals, this might not matter—a sandal contains no original meaning. There is nothing to lose. However, the Ten Commandments and the Columbine shooting are done a great disservice when they become secondary to a political agenda. By so denigrating the Ten Commandments, the Christian Right not only defiles what is most holy about them but also effectively throws sand in the face of the public, obscuring the very real consequences of displaying them in public schools.

WORKS CITED

Henderson, Charles. (2001, April 4). About Christianity http://www.christianity.about. com/religion/christianity/library/weekly/aa062299.htm

Nietzsche, F. (1999). On truth and lying in a non-moral sense. In R. Guess & R. Speirs (Eds),. The Birth of Tragedy and Other Writings. Cambridge, UK: Cambridge University Press.

People for the American Way. (2001, April 4). http://www.pfaw.org

Shoes of the fisherman (2001, April 4). Shoes of the fisherman. http://www.shoes of the fisherman.com

Teva (2001, April 4, 17). http://www.teva.com

Suggested Readings

Bartholomae, D. (1985). Inventing the university. In Rose, M. (Ed.), *When a writer can't write*. New York: Guildford Press.

Bartholomae, D. (February 1995). Writing with teachers: A conversation with Peter Elbow. *CCC, 46*, 62–71.

Berlin, J. A. (Fall, 1992). Poststructuralism, cultural studies, and the composition classroom. *Rhetoric review, 11*, 16–33.

Berlin, J. A. (September, 1988). Rhetoric and ideology in the writing class. *CE, 50*, 477–494.

Bizzell, P., & Herzberg, B. (1991). *The Bedford bibliography for teachers of writing*. New York: Bedford Books.

Black, L. J. (1998). *Between talk and teaching*: Reconsidering the writing conference. Logan, UT: Utah State University Press.

DiYanni, R., & Hoy, P. C. (2000). *Encounters: Essays for exploration and inquiry*.

DiYanni, R., & Hoy, P. C. (2004). *The Scribner handbook for writers* (Fourth Ed.). New York: Longman Press.

Elbow, P. (1973). *Writing without teachers*. New York: Oxford University Press.

Elbow, P. (1986). *Embracing contraries: Explorations in learning and teaching*. New York: Oxford University Press.

Enos, T. (1987). *A sourcebook for basic writing teachers*. New York: Random House.

Freire, P. (1981). *Pedagogy of the oppressed*. (M. B. Ramos, Trans.). New York: Continuum.

Hoy, P. C. (1992). *Reading and writing essays: The imaginative task*. New York: McGraw Hill.

Lawson, B., S. S. Ryan, & W. R. Winterowd. (1989). *Encountering student texts: Interpretive issues in reading student writing*. Urbana, IL: National Council of Teachers of English.

Leki, I. (1992). *Understanding ESL writers: A guide for teachers*. Portsmouth, N.H.: Boynton/Cook Publishers.

Petrosky, A. R., & D. Bartholomae, eds. (1986) *The teaching of writing: Eighty-fifth yearbook of the national society for the study of education, part II*. Chicago: Univ. of Chicago Press.

Tate, G., E. P., Corbett, J., & Myers, N. (1994). *The writing teacher's sourcebook*, 3rd ed. New York: Oxford University Press.

Shaughnessy, M. P. (1977). *Errors and expectations*. Oxford: Oxford University Press.

Summerfield, J., & Summerfield, G. (1986). *Texts and contexts: A contribution to the theory and practice of teaching composition*. New York: Random House.

Villanueva, Jr., V. (Ed.) (1997). *Cross-talk in comp theory: A reader*. Urbana, IL: National Council of Teachers of English.

Welch, N. (1997). *Getting restless: Rethinking revision in writing instruction*. Portsmouth, N.H.: Boynton/Cook Publishers.

Winterowd, W. R. (with J. Blum). (1994). *A teacher's introduction to composition in the rhetorical tradition*. Urbana, IL: National Council of Teachers of English.

References

Adorno, Theodor and Horkeimer, Max. (1997). The culture industry. In *Dialectic of Enlightenment*. (J. Cumming, Trans.). New York: Continuum.

Anzaldua, G. (2000). How to tame a wild tongue. In P. C. Hoy II & R. DiYanni (Eds.), *Encounters: Essays for exploration and inquiry* (pp. 265–275). New York: McGraw-Hill.

Bachelard, G. (1994). *The poetics of space* (M. Jolas, Trans.). Boston: Beacon.

Barthes, R. (1977). *Image music text* (S. Heath, Trans.). New York: Hill and Wang.

Barthes, R. (1981). *Camera lucida* (R. Howard, Trans.). New York: Hill and Wang.

Barthes, R. (1994). Leaving the movie theatre. In P. Lopate, *The art of the personal essay* (pp. 418–422). New York: Bantam.

Baudrillard, J. (1983). *Simulations*. (P. Foss, P. Patton, & P. Beitchman, Trans.). New York: Semiotext(e).

Bentham, J. (1995). *The panopticon writings*. New York: Verso.

Berger, J. (1995). *Ways of seeing*. New York: Viking.

Brecht, B. (1992). *Brecht on theatre: the development of an aesthetic* (J. Willett, Ed. & Trans.). New York: Hill and Wang.

Butler, J. (1993). *Bodies that matter: on the discursive limits of "sex."* London: Routledge.

Clayton, M. (2002, October 1). New models for higher education. *Christian Science Monitor*. (Retrieved from http://www.csmonitor.com/2002/1001/plls02–html)

Cooper, B. (2000). Burl's. In P. C. Hoy II & R. DiYanni (Eds.), *Encounters: Essays for exploration and inquiry* (pp. 153–162). New York: McGraw-Hill.

Dillard, A. (1999). Total eclipse. In *Teaching a stone to talk: Expeditions and encounters.* New York: HarperCollins.

Edmundson, M. (1997, September). On the uses of a liberal education. *Harper's Magazine*. (pp. 39–49).

Ellison, R. (1980). *Invisible man*. New York: Random House.

Etchells, T. (1999). *Certain fragments*. New York: Routledge.

Fine, M. (1991). *Framing dropouts: Notes on the politics of a public high school*. Albany: State University of New York Press.

Fish, S. (2002, June 21). Say it ain't so. *The Chronicle of Higher Education*. (Retrieved from http://chronicle.com/jobs/2002/06/2002062101c.htm.)

Fiske, J. (1996). Popular culture. In F. Lentriccia & T. McLaughlin (Eds.), *Critical terms for literacy study* (pp. 321–335). Chicago: University of Chicago Press.

Fussell, P. (2000). Indy. In P. C. Hoy II & R. DiYanni (Eds.), *Encounters: Essays for exploration and inquiry* (pp. 265–275). New York: McGraw-Hill.

Gilman, C. P. (1989). Women and economics. In *The yellow wallpaper and other writings*. New York: Bantam.

Girard, R. (1977). *Violence and the sacred* (P. Gregory, Trans.). Baltimore: Johns Hopkins. (Original work published in 1972)

Gladwell, M. (1997). The coolhunt. (Retrieved from http://www.gladwell.com/1997/1997_03_17_1_cod.htm)

Goodman, B. (Director). (2001). *Frontline: Merchants of cool*. Boston: WBGH Boston.

Gonzalaz, M. Houston, & Chen, V. (Eds.). *Our voices: Essays in culture, ethnicity, and communication*. Los Angeles: Roxbury.

Greenblatt, S. (1996). Culture. In F. Lentricchia & T. McLaughlin (Eds.), *Critical terms for literary study* (pp. 225–232). Chicago: University of Chicago Press.

Harper, P. B. (1999). *Private affairs: Critical ventures in the culture of social relations*. New York: New York University Press.

Hartman, S. (1996). *Scenes of subjection*. Oxford: Oxford University Press.

hooks, b. (1994). *Teaching to transgress: Education as the practice of freedom*. London: Routledge.

Kavanaugh, J. (1996). Popular culture. In F. Lentricchia & T. McLaughlin (Eds.), *Critical terms for literary study* (pp. 306–320). Chicago: University of Chicago.

Kincaid, J. (2000). On seeing England for the first time. In P. C. Hoy II & R. DiYanni (Eds.), *Encounters: Essays for exploration and inquiry* (pp. 362–371). New York: McGraw-Hill.

King, M. L., Jr. (2000). Letter from Birmingham jail. In P. C. Hoy II & R. DiYanni (Eds.), *Encounters: Essays for exploration and inquiry* (pp. 372–385). New York: McGraw-Hill.

Lozano, Elizabeth. (2000). The cultural experience of space and body. In A. Gonzolez, M. Houston, & V. Chen (Eds.), *Our voices: Essays in culture, ethnicity, and communication* (pp. 218–234). Los Angeles: Roxbury.

McKibben, Bill. (2003, April). The posthuman condition. *Harper's Magazine, 306*, 15–19.

Milton, J. (2001) (C. Ricks, Ed.). *Paradise lost*. New York: Signet.

Morrison, T. (2000). The site of memory. In P. C. Hoy II & R. DiYanni (Eds.)., *Encounters: Essays for exploration and inquiry* (pp. 428–438). New York: McGraw-Hill.

Nietzsche, F. (1993). *Human, all too human* (R. J. Hollingdale, Trans.). Cambridge: Cambridge University Press. (Original work published 1886)

Nietzsche, F. (1999). On truth and lying in a non-moral sense (R. Guess & R. Speirs, Eds. and Trans.). *The birth of tragedy and other writings* (pp. 141–153). Cambridge: Cambridge University Press.

Office of Educational Research and Improvement. (2000). *Digest of education statistics*. Washington, D.C.: Congressional Information Service.

Orwell, G. (2000). Marrakech. In P. C. Hoy II & R. DiYanni (Eds.), *Encounters: Essays for exploration and inquiry* (pp. 451–457). New York: McGraw-Hill.

Pollock, G. (1994). Feminism/Foucault—Surveillance/sexuality. In N. Bryson, M. A. Holly, & K. Moxey (Eds.), *Visual culture* (pp. 1–41). Middleton, CT: Wesleyan University Press.

Rodriguez, R. (2000a). Late victorians. In P. C. Hoy II & R. DiYanni (Eds.), *Encounters: Essays for exploration and inquiry* (pp. 493–505). New York: McGraw-Hill.

Rodriguez, R. (2000b). The achievement of desire. In P. C. Hoy II & R. DiYanni (Eds.), *Encounters: Essays for exploration and inquiry* (pp. 474–492). New York: McGraw-Hill.

Stein, G. (1975). *How to write*. New York: Dover.

Talbot, M. (2000). *Les tres riches heures de* Martha Stewart. In P. C. Hoy II & R. DiYanni (Eds.), *Encounters: Essays for exploration and inquiry* (pp. 592–601). New York: McGraw-Hill.

Tarantino, Q. (Director). (1994). *Pulp fiction*. New York: Miramax Films.

Taylor, M. (1999). *About religion*. Chicago: University of Chicago Press.

Turner, V. (1969). *The ritual process*. New York: Penguin.

Wachowski, A., & Wachowski, L. (Directors). (1999). *The matrix*. Burbank: Warner Home Video.

Weaver, C. (1996). *Creating support for effective literacy education*. Portsmouth, NH: Heinemann.

White, E. B. (2000). Once more to the lake. In P. C. Hoy II & R. DiYanni (Ed.), *Encounters: Essays for exploration and inquiry* (pp. 723–727). New York: McGraw-Hill.

Zizek, S. (1995). *The sublime object of ideology*. New York: Verso.

Zizek, S. (2000). *The plague of fantasies*. New York: Verso.

Index

About the Authors

Kristin Dombek teaches writing and literature at New York University and Barnard College. She is finishing a Ph.D. at NYU, and writing a dissertation about the popular culture of the Christian Right.

Scott Herndon is completing a Ph.D. in English at New York University, where he is writing a dissertation on globalization, cosmopolitanism, and Hemingway. He teaches writing at NYU, Eugene Lang College, and Urban Word NYC. He is co-author of *Brave New Voices: The Youth Speaks Guide to Teaching Spoken Word Poetry* (Heinemann, 2001), and his writing has appeared in the *Brooklyn Rail* and *Teachers and Writers Magazine*. He is finishing his first novel.